Aprendo a leer y escribir
Teaching Guide

How to Teach to Read and Write in Spanish with a Phonetic Syllabic Method

Mónica Sarmiento

Published by Mónica Sarmiento
E-mail: mssarmiento@hotmail.com
Menlo Park, CA 94025

Copyright © 2020, Mónica Sarmiento

All rights reserved. No part of this book may be reproduced
in any form or by any electronic or mechanical means.

Library of Congress Cataloging-in-Publication Data

Mónica Sarmiento, Author
Andrea Corradini, Book Designer
Agustina Lopes, Cover Designer

ISBN: 978-1-7346665-7-1
Printed in the United States of America. First Edition

Teacher's Guide Structure

SECTION I
Introduction .... pg. 7
Intended Audience .... pg. 7
Instructional Method .... pg. 8
Teaching Principles .... pg. 9
Implementation Guidelines .... pg. 9
Instructional Process .... pg. 10

SECTION II
IMPLEMENTATION: LESSON SAMPLES .... pg. 11

SECTION III
SUPPLEMENTAL ACTIVITIES
Phonological Awareness and Materialization Techniques .... pg. 31
1. **Syllable Awareness Techniques** .... pg. 32
2. **Syllable Segmentation** .... pg. 33
2.1. Clapping out Syllables .... pg. 33
2.2. Written Words Syllable Division .... pg. 34
3. **Phoneme Segmentation** .... pg. 34
3.1. Stretching out the Sounds in Words .... pg. 34
3.2. Finger Spelling .... pg. 35
3.3. Finger Tapping for Segmenting .... pg. 35
3.4. Elkonin Boxes .... pg. 37
4. **Syllable Blending** .... pg. 37
4.1. Syllable Blending .... pg. 37
4.2. Syllable-Phoneme Blending .... pg. 38
5. **Phoneme Blending** .... pg. 38
5.1. Oral Phoneme Blending .... pg. 38
5.2. Finger Tapping for Blending .... pg. 39
6. **Guided Word Building** .... pg. 39
6.1. Making Words for Spelling Practice .... pg. 39
6.2. Making Words for Reading Practice .... pg. 40
6.3. Making Words for Reading with Letter Substitution .... pg. 41
6.4. Making Syllables for Spelling Practice .... pg. 41
6.5. Making Syllables for Reading Practice .... pg. 42
7. **Spelling** .... pg. 42
7.1. Spelling Syllables .... pg. 42
7.2. Spelling Words .... pg. 43
7.3. Share Spelling .... pg. 43

TEACHER'S GUIDE STRUCTURE

SECTION IV
UNIT'S LEARNING PLAN .... pg. 45
1. Scope for **INTENSIVE** Instruction .... pg. 47
2. Scope for **READING INTERVENTION** Instruction .... pg. 53
3. Scope for **AT GRADE LEVEL** Instruction .... pg. 59
4. Scope for **ACCELERATED** Instruction .... pg. 65

SECTION V
ASSESSMENT INSTRUMENT .... pg. 69
1. Teacher's Protocol (Books 1-5) .... pg. 72
2. Student's Protocol (Books 1-5) .... pg. 83
3. Teacher's Protocol (Books 6-7) .... pg. 117
4. Student's Protocol (Books 6-7) .... pg. 119

STUDENT PROGRESS CHART .... pg. 107
1. For **Teachers** .... pg. 107
2. For **Students** .... pg. 109

SCREENER: SYLLABIC PHONICS ASSESSMENT .... pg. 111
1. Teacher's Protocol (Books 1-5) .... pg. 111
2. Student's Protocol (Books 1-5) .... pg. 113

APPENDIX BOOK 6 AND BOOK 7 .... pg. 115

SECTION I

- INTRODUCTION
- INTENDED AUDIENCE
- INSTRUCTIONAL METHOD
- TEACHING PRINCIPLES
- IMPLEMENTATION GUIDELINES
- INSTRUCTIONAL PROCESS

Teaching Guide
Phonetic Syllabic Method

Introduction

Aprendo a leer y escribir is a program designed to teach children how to read and write in Spanish using a phonetic-syllabic approach. The program consists of five workbooks that help students learn through a series of carefully thought out and well-sequenced activities.

The Teaching Guide was developed to help educational professionals and parents implement the program and use **Aprendo a leer y escribir** effectively with their students. The Teaching Guide provides detailed instructions in the form of scripted activities for each of the lessons in the student workbook. In addition, the Teaching Guide includes a wealth of supplemental activities, as well as syllabi (suggestions for scoping and sequencing the lessons) for different learner profiles and educational settings.

With its emphasis on the syllable as the basic unit of reading instruction and the letter-sound associations that define this unit, the phonetic-syllabic approach is particularly well suited to teach reading and writing in Spanish. The reasons are twofold:

   1. Spanish is an alphabetic language. This means that there is a near-perfect correspondence between the sounds of the language and the letters that represent those sounds. Students of Spanish can easily infer the sounds of words based on their orthographic representation.

   2. Spanish is a syllabic language. A syllable is a sound unit that can be easily learned. Syllables are easier for children to pronounce and to recognize than the letters of the alphabet. For this reason, teaching children to read Spanish by teaching letters in isolation is ineffective.

Intended Audience

Aprendo a leer y escribir targets children from kindergarten through 1st grade, as well as children with learning differences. The program can be used with both first and second-language learners of Spanish in bilingual or dual immersion programs.

The program can be taught by any teacher, whether in a general or special education setting. The workbook activities are easy enough to use with the instructions provided in the Teaching Guide that even non-specialists such as parents or teacher's assistants can successfully teach reading with this program.

Instructional Method

 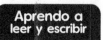

Aprendo a leer y escribir is based on a *phonetic-syllabic method* that has been developed and refined by the author in over thirty years of teaching children Spanish reading and writing in a variety of settings. The phonetic-syllabic approach proposed here can be described as a synthetic-phonic method of reading instruction. Students are taught groups of letter-sound associations or *syllables*. Syllables are the basic building blocks that students learn to manipulate by creatively combining them with other syllables to create new words.

Because the syllable is considered the basic sound unit of reading instruction, the concept of phonological awareness plays a key role in the learning process. Phonological awareness is a broad term that includes word awareness, syllable awareness, and phonemic awareness. Children must first acquire the ability to identify and manipulate the syllables that makeup words (*syllabic awareness*) before they can learn to manipulate individual sounds (*phonemes*), the smallest units of speech (*phonemic awareness*).

A syllable can be perceived and produced in isolation. This is why **Aprendo a leer y escribir** emphasizes developing children's syllabic awareness first. Once established, syllabic awareness allows the learner to become aware of phonemes, a fundamental fact for the acquisition of reading and writing. (Clemente M. y Dominguez A. 1999)(1)

Aprendo a leer y escribir is based on phonics, which raises the question how phonics relates to phonemic awareness. Phonemic awareness and phonics are not the same. Phonemic awareness is the ability to manipulate sounds in words, ORALLY. Phonics involves the connections between PRINTED letters and speech sounds. These are two essential and closely related aspects necessary for reading.

The **Aprendo a leer y escribir Teaching Guide** includes scripted lessons' samples for the workbooks and a series of supplemental activities designed to develop students' syllabic and phonemic awareness. The supplemental activities include materialization techniques that build and reinforce young children's awareness of words, syllables, and phonemes through the use of tangible objects or physical actions (use of elastic bands for stretching out sounds, finger tapping, etc). [1] The materialization techniques presented in **Aprendo a leer y escribir** are organized in a sequence of progressive difficulty.

Phonological awareness instruction and materialization techniques are essential for establishing the mental connection between sounds and letters which Marilyn Adams has called the "alphabetic principle". In her book *Beginning to Read* she claims that *"perhaps the single most important goal in giving students a productive knowledge of letter-sound correspondences is to convey to them the basic alphabetic principle.*" (Adams, Marilyn. 1990)(2)
This principle could be called the essence of learning to read.

(1) Clemente, M. y Dominguez, A. (1999). *La enseñanza de la lectura: enfoque psicolingüístico y sociocultural.* Madrid: Pirámide.
(2) Marilyn Jager Adams (1990). *Beginning to read: Thinking and Learning about Print.* Cambridge, MA: MIT Press.
[1] Materialization uses a tangible object and/ or physical action to represent a mental construct such as a sound or word part and or whole words. (Gentry 2004). Materialization techniques grew out of Vygotskian theory and research (Bodrova and Leong 1998, Vygotsky 1978). There are several resourceful materialization techniques especially useful for working with beginning readers and writers.

TEACHING PRINCIPLES • IMPLEMENTATION GUIDELINES

Teaching Principles

The **Aprendo a leer y escribir** approach is based on a series of teaching principles that have been shown to be highly effective in different educational settings.

- **Systematic Instruction:** Aprendo a leer y escribir provides a carefully planned sequence of instructional activities that identifies and selects the most efficient means to maximize learning.

- **Progression:** Aprendo a leer y escribir provides a progression of modeled, guided, and independent teaching strategies. First, the teacher models the activity by explicitly and directly introducing a new syllable. Then, as needed, the teacher adds an explicit explanation, scaffolding students with just enough teaching aids to enable them to succeed. During this phase, the teacher corrects student errors and provides feedback. Finally, students work more independently, applying what they've just learned in new contexts.

- **Well-sequenced activities:** The student activities provided for each newly introduced syllable are sequenced in a manner that supports and optimizes the program's overall learning objectives.

- **Cumulative learning effect:** Activities build on each other. Students are encouraged to combine new syllables with previously learned syllables to make new words.

- **Syllable coverage:** In the course of the program, students learn twenty-two discrete syllables consisting of a consonant and a vowel. The most frequent syllables are introduced first, thereby maximizing the number of words students are able to read in a relatively short period of time.

- **Syllable placement:** Aprendo a leer y escribir introduces a new syllable always in words where the syllable appears in an initial position. This principle is applied consistently throughout the material. It makes the auditory discrimination, reproduction, and memorization of the syllable much easier than if the syllable was positioned in the middle or at the end of a word.

- **Vocabulary coverage:** Aprendo a leer y escribir introduces new words with each new syllable. Every new word introduced in the workbooks has an image as visual support to facilitate the children's understanding of each word that they read. Words are repeated throughout the book, which facilitates their memorization, and thus the enrichment of the child's vocabulary. By the end of the program, students will have learned 500 new words.

Implementation Guidelines

Aprendo a leer y escribir can be implemented in the following educational settings:

1. General Education: Aprendo a leer y escribir provides all students with a foundation for reading and writing. When used with the supplemental activities included in this guide, **Aprendo a leer y escribir**, promotes phonological awareness, decoding abilities, vocabulary acquisition,

INSTRUCTIONAL PROCESS

as well as handwriting and spelling skills. In a general educational setting, the phonics-based reading program of **Aprendo a leer y escribir** should be combined with a core literacy program or a literature and language arts program for a comprehensive approach to teaching reading and writing.

2. Reading Intervention: Aprendo a leer y escribir is well suited to be used by reading specialists in small individualized group settings to support children who are struggling with learning to read and write.

3. Special Education: Aprendo a leer y escribir is well suited to help students with a language-based disability to master basic reading and literacy skills.

Instructional Process

Aprendo a Leer y Escribir, comprises a series of five workbooks, each of which covers the following letters. **Book 1:** Vowels AEIOU; **Book 2:** M P S L T; **Book 3:** R N B F D; **Book 4:** C (ca, co, cu) C (ce, ci) que, qui; J G (ga, go, gu) G (ge, gi, gue, gui) CH; **Book 5:** V LL Y Z H K W X.

Following the phonetic-syllabic method the program starts by introducing each of the five vowels. Then, syllables are introduced by combining each consonant with each of the vowels to form a direct syllable (consonant + vowel). Once children command a syllable, they are ready to combine it with another one to make a new word. This pattern repeats throughout the program. By the end of the program, the child will be able to read and write any word with two or more direct syllables.

The following recommendations should be followed when using **Aprendo a leer y escribir**:

• Kindergarten teachers should start with book 1, teaching the vowels.

• Reading intervention teachers or special education teachers should establish a baseline of what students already know to determine the starting point for instruction. An assessment tool is provided in this guide, but any curriculum-based assessment instrument (BBA) can be used. It is highly recommended to use formative assessment during the learning process, to help teachers adjust pacing and include more supplemental activities if needed.

• The assessment instrument provided in this guide allows the teacher to **(1)** determine the phonics learning goals for the struggling student, **(2)** monitor the student's progress, and **(3)** group students according to their phonics learning needs.

SECTION II

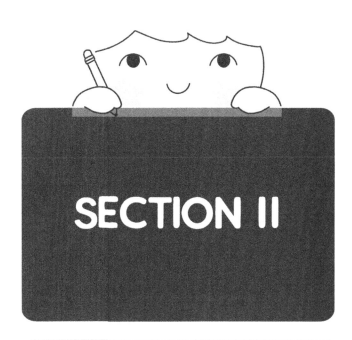

IMPLEMENTATION

LESSON SAMPLES

Teaching Guide
Phonetic Syllabic Method

IMPLEMENTATION: **LESSON SAMPLES**

Lesson #1, book 1

GOAL: Explicit Teaching of Vowel A a

A
a

Activity #1

The student identifies all of the pictures that have the same initial vowel.

Say:

"Esta letra es la letra "a" y dice /a/."
"Veamos estos dibujos y escuchemos con atención con qué letra empiezan todos ellos.
Este es un ...aaavión. Digan la palabra aaavión, empieza con /a/." Lo coloreamos (o redondeamos) porque empieza con /a/.

Do:

You point to the first picture. You model the "a" sound by stretching the vowel sound and saying it with a higher tone of voice.
You proceed with the rest of the pictures as with the word "avión".

PRACTICE TIP:

- You can always expand the lesson to develop further vocabulary and understanding of words. When introducing words, talk with the students about that new word/concept. For example, when introducing the word "avión" you can expand talking about planes or students' personal experiences. You can also tell a short fictional story about planes. If time is limited just focus on the phonics aspect of the words.

Activity #2

In this activity, the student practices letter formation through tracing with different degrees of support.

IMPLEMENTATION: **LESSON SAMPLES**

 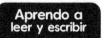

Say:

"Vamos a practicar escribir la letra A mayúscula. Colocamos el lápiz en el punto, luego trazamos una línea hacia abajo, volvemos a colocar el lápiz en el punto y trazamos otra línea hacia abajo luego trazamos una pequeña línea a través."

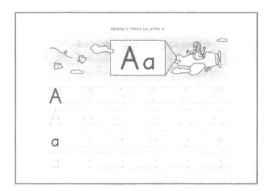

Do:

You demonstrate the letter formation on a lined board or in the same workbook while talking through it.

- First you model and the student observes. You describe each step of what you are doing while writing the letter.
- Second, the student imitates. Students should do what you are doing at the same time as you are. The student also should describe what you are doing.
- The next step is copying. As you might see this activity in **Aprendo a leer y escribir** offers different degrees of support. On the first line, the student traces over a dotted line, on the second line, only the vertices of the letters are marked so that the student can be guided by them.
- This pattern repeats with uppercase and lowercase letters. Finally, students can have extra practice on a lined whiteboard or paper.

PRACTICE TIP:

- It is important to teach letter formation, by practicing tracing with correct directionality. It helps the student to memorize (kinetic memory) the letter.

Activity #3

The student identifies and discriminates words that begin with the target initial sound.

Say:

*"Veamos estos dibujos y escuchemos con atención con qué letra comienza cada uno de ellos.
Vamos a colorear (o redondear) sólo los dibujos que comienzan con la letra /A/. Algunos de estos dibujos no comienzan con la letra /A/.
Este es un? ...eeelefante. Digan la palabra.
"eeelefante, comienza con aaa? No.
Esta es una?....mmmmanzana, comienza con aaa? No.
Este es un?....aaavión, comienza con aaa? Sí.
Redondeamos (o coloreamos) avión".*

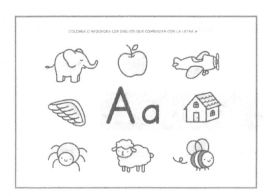

IMPLEMENTATION: **LESSON SAMPLES**

Do:

You point to the elephant. You say "elefante" extending the /e/ sound.
You continue pointing to the rest of the pictures and repeating the same script.

Activity #4

In this activity, students develop visual discrimination and letter recognition in their uppercase and lowercase forms.

Say:

"Colorea las mariposas que tengan la "A" mayúscula."

Say:

"Colorea los honguitos que tengan la "a" minúscula."

Activity #5

Students practice to auditorily discriminate the initial target sound. They also practice letter formation.

Say:

"Esta es la letra "A" mayúscula y dice /a/ y esta es la letra "a" minúscula. Tomen un lápiz y tracemos las letras para practicar su escritura.

Do:

You point to letter "A" and "a" and ask students to trace the letters.

IMPLEMENTATION: **LESSON SAMPLES**

Say:

Vamos a nombrar cada uno de estos dibujos y escuchar con atención cuáles de ellos empiezan con /a/. ¿Qué es esto? ...Pájaro, pájaro empieza con.... /a/? No. ¿Qué es esto?...Avión, avión comienza con /a/? Sí, entonces lo redondeamos (o coloreamos) Qué es esto?... Nube, nube comienza con /a/? No. Continuemos con la línea siguiente..."

Do:

You point to one picture at a time and ask the student what it is. You confirm their correct answer. You ask the student to listen carefully and circle or color the things that begin with the target sound, in this case /a/.
You continue using the same script with the following pictures.

> **PRACTICE TIPS:**
> - When possible, say the word stretching the first sound.
> - You can choose to color or circle the correct picture, depending on how much time you want to allocate to this activity.

Activity #6

Game. Students practice saying words that begin with the target syllable.

Say:

"Ayuda a la abeja como llegar hasta el panal. Necesitas un amigo y un dado. Nombra los dibujos mientras avanzas (o nombra el dibujo de la casilla a la que llegas)"

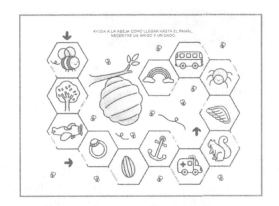

Do:

Students play the game in pairs. They throw a dice and move along the board. They can name all of the images while moving through the spaces or they can only name the pictures where they land.

> **YOU CONTINUE USING THE SAME SCRIPT AS FOR THE LETTER Aa WITH THE REST OF THE VOWELS IN BOOK 1.**

Aprendo a leer y escribir

IMPLEMENTATION: **LESSON SAMPLES**

After each vowel is introduced and practiced, there is an activity worksheet that has the objective of reviewing the vowel sounds already learned.

Here is a lesson sample for those activities.

A-E-I-O-U PRACTICE

Activity a/e

This activity helps students practice listening, auditory discriminating and matching the initial sound with the correct letter. (pg.13, 20, 27, 34)

Say:

"Traza la letra con la que comienza cada imagen. ¿Qué es? Si aaaraña comienza con…?
(student says /a/), **traza la letra "a" de araña."**

Do:

You point to the first image, spider and ask the student to name the picture. You say the word stretching the first sound. The student matches the sound with the correct letter and traces it.

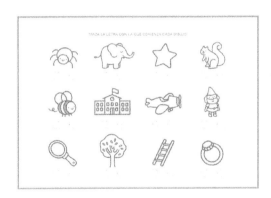

> **PRACTICE TIP:**
> - You continue using the same script for a few more images and then guide the rest of the practice.

Use the same script with the following activities.

Activity a/e/i/o/u

The student practices identifying and spelling the first vowel sound of a word. (pg.35)

Say:

"Escribe la letra con la que comienza cada dibujo. ¿Qué es? Ancla. ¿Ancla empieza con…? A. Escriban la letra "a" en la línea debajo del dibujo".

Do:

You point to the first image, "anchor" and ask the student to name it. You say the word stretching the first sound. The student writes the initial sound of the word in between the lines.

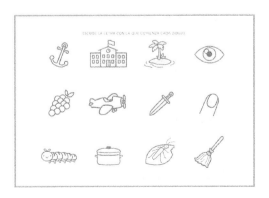

II - 17

IMPLEMENTATION: **LESSON SAMPLES**

> **PRACTICE TIP:**
> - If you feel confident that students can continue working independently, you should let them continue by themselves. Although, sometimes you might need to keep scaffolding the activity with some of the students.

Activity a/e/i/o/u

The student practices identifying the first vowel sound of a word and matching it with the correct letter. (pg. 36)

Say:

"Di el nombre del dibujo y conectalo con la letra inicial. ¿Qué es? Uvas, ¿Uvas empieza con a? i? u? uuuvas, si con /u/ conecta el dibujo con una línea con la letra /u/".

Do:

You point to the first image, "grapes" and ask students to name it. You say the word stretching the first sound. The student connects with a line the image with the initial letter.

Activity a/e/i/o/u

Categorization; student sorts images by its initial sound. Students compare words by their initial sound so that they categorize similar sounds and associate them consistently with letters, in this case the vowels.

Say:

"Recorta los dibujos, agrúpalos según su letra inicial en la página siguiente".

Do:

Students need to cut out the pictures from page 37 and paste them on page 38. Students sort pictures by its initial sound. Students work independently.

Aprendo a leer y escribir

IMPLEMENTATION: **LESSON SAMPLES**

Activity a/e/i/o/u

Game. Students practice reading the vowels and saying words that begin with all the different vowels. Students work on initial sound discrimination and they practice vocabulary.

Say:

"Necesitas un amigo y un dado. Nombra las vocales mientras avanzas (o nombra la vocal de la casilla a la que llegas)"

Do:

Students play the game in pairs. They throw a dice and move along the board. They can name all of the vowels while moving through the spaces or they can only name the vowel where they land.

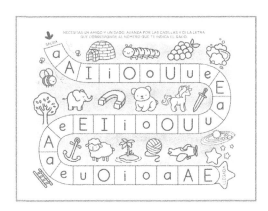

PRACTICE TIPS:

- An extension for this game to practice vocabulary, is that students can name a word that begins with the vowel where they landed.
- The board game has all the pictures from the previous lessons displayed around and can be used as clues.

IMPLEMENTATION: **LESSON SAMPLES**

Lesson #1, book 2

GOAL: Explicit Teaching of Syllables: **ma, me, mi, mo, mu**

M m

Activity #1

The students identify all of the pictures that have the same initial sound.

Say:

Esta letra es la "eme" y dice /m/. Veamos estos dibujos y escuchemos con atención con qué letra empiezan todos ellos. Las palabras que empiezan con /m/ las coloreamos (o redondeamos).
Esta es "mamá", ¿quién es? /mmmmaaamá/.
Empieza con /m/, la coloreamos (o redondeamos).

Do:

You point to the first picture. You model the syllable sound "ma" by stretching the /m/ sound.
You proceed with the rest of the pictures as with the word "mamá".

PRACTICE TIP:
- You can always expand the lesson to develop further vocabulary and understanding of words. When introducing words, talk with the students about that new word or concept. For example, when introducing the word "mono" you can talk about what monkeys eat, where do they live, etc. If time is limited just focus on the phonics aspect of the words.

Activity #2

In this activity, the student practices letter formation through tracing with different degrees of support.

Say:

"Vamos a practicar escribir la letra M mayúscula. Colocamos el lápiz en el punto, luego trazamos una línea hacia abajo, volvemos a colocar el lápiz en el punto y trazamos otra línea hacia abajo luego otra hacia arriba y abajo una vez más."

IMPLEMENTATION: **LESSON SAMPLES**

Do:

You demonstrate the letter formation on a lined board or in the same workbook while talking through it.

- First you model and the student observes. You describe each step of what you are doing while writing the letter.
- Second, the student imitates. Students should do what you are doing at the same time as you are. The student also should describe what you are doing.
- The next step is copying. As you might see this activity in **Aprendo a leer y escribir** offers different degrees of support. On the first line, the student traces over a dotted line, on the second line, only the vertices of the letters are marked so that the student can be guided by them.
- This pattern repeats with uppercase and lowercase letters. Finally, students can have extra practice on a lined whiteboard or paper.

PRACTICE TIP:
- It is important to teach letter formation, by practicing tracing with correct directionality. It helps the student to memorize (kinetic memory) the letter.

Activity #3

The student identifies and discriminates words that begin with the target initial syllable.

Say:

"*Veamos estos dibujos y escuchemos con atención con qué letra empieza cada uno de ellos. Vamos a redondear (o colorear) solo los dibujos que comienzan con la letra "m" /m/. Algunos de estos dibujos no empiezan con /m/".*
"*Esta es una /mmmaaanzana/
Digan la palabra conmigo, /mmmaaanzana/ comienza con /mmm/ /mmmaaa/, entonces redondeamos (o coloreamos) la manzana".*

Do:

You point to the apple. You say the name of the picture extending the initial sound. You continue the same way with the rest of the pictures.

IMPLEMENTATION: **LESSON SAMPLES**

Activity #4

In this activity, students develop visual discrimination and letter recognition in their uppercase and lowercase forms.

Say:

Colorea los espacios con las letras "M" mayúscula y "m" minúscula y descubrirás un dibujo que comienza con /m/…

Do:

You point to the letters "M" and "m" on the book, explaining which one is upper-case and lower-case. (The children will discover a picture of a bow "moño").

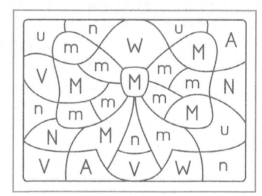

Activity #5

The student names a picture, then sounds out the first two letters that make the initial syllable and finally blends the two sounds together.

Say:

Di el nombre de este dibujo…"Mano" acá dice /m/ /a/ todo junto /ma/ de mano. Tracemos las letras que forman la sílaba /ma/. Escribimos /ma/ sobre esta línea. Las palabras están formadas de partes más pequeñas que se llaman sílabas. La palabra "mano" tiene dos sílabas: /ma/ /no/ (you clap each syllable), la primera sílaba de "mano" es "ma", mano comienza con /ma/. El siguiente dibujo es…"mesa".

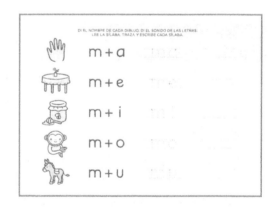

Do:

You point to the picture of the "hand". Then you point to the letters "m" and "a". You explain what is a syllable and clap while saying each syllable. Finally you show the students where to write the syllable "ma".

PRACTICE TIPS:

- It is recommended that you model the whole activity, since it is the first activity that explicitly teaches the syllable.
- You can use other supplemental activities to help develop syllable awareness. See Supplemental activities section in this guide.

IMPLEMENTATION: **LESSON SAMPLES**

Activity #6

The student names the different pictures and establishes the one on one correspondence between the initial syllable sound and its written representation.

Say:

Di el nombre del dibujo y únelo con la sílaba inicial correspondiente. ¿Qué es? "Mono", /mmooono/ comienza con /mo/. Donde dice /mo/, tracemos sobre esta línea para llegar a /mo/.

Do:

You point to the picture of the monkey. Encourage the students to name the picture. You say the word slowly, stretching the first syllable. You model how to connect the picture to the initial syllable.

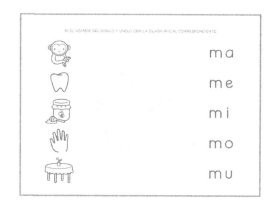

PRACTICE TIP:
- You can continue with a few more words but then encourage the students to work independently, with the rest of the items.

Activity #7

In this activity, the student needs to visually discriminate the consonant and vowel that makes the target syllable in its correct sequence.

Say:

Colorea los globos que tengan las mismas sílabas que los niños. ¿Qué dice aca? /ma/.
Escuchen atentamente /m/ (pause) /a/, en la sílaba /ma/, primero está la /m/ y luego la /a/, ahora busquemos los globos que tengan la sílaba /ma/ en el orden correcto.

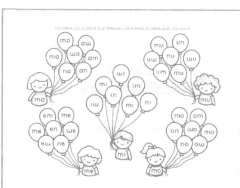

Do:

You point to the girl with the syllable /ma/ on her t-shirt. Then point to each of the balloons and help the student to compare and pay attention to the sequence of the letters that makes /ma/. Model the first syllable and let the students to work on their own with the rest of the items.

PRACTICE TIP:
- The teacher models the first syllable "ma" and students continue with the rest of the items independently.

IMPLEMENTATION: **LESSON SAMPLES**

Activity #8

The student names the picture, isolates the first syllable from the rest of the word, and matches the sound with the correct syllable.

Say:

Di el nombre del dibujo y redondea la sílaba inicial que corresponda. ¿Qué es? Sí, es mesa. Mesa comienza con…? Me… veamos donde dice /me/, leamos juntos, ma, me, mo, si acá dice /me/. Redondeamos /me/.

Do:

You point to the picture and to each of the different syllables. You help to scaffold the activity, as needed.

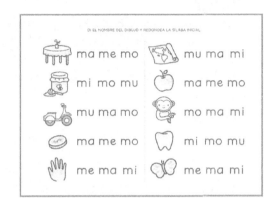

Activity #9

The student reads the syllable to be learned and matches the picture(s) that begins with that syllable.

Say:

Vamos a leer y trazar cada sílaba, luego redondean el dibujo que comienza con la sílaba que corresponde. Comencemos por leer esta sílaba. ¿Qué dice aca? Muy bien, /ma/. Tracemos con el lápiz la sílaba /ma/. Ahora redondeamos aquellos dibujos que comienzan con /ma/, repitan /ma/. ¿Qué es? Si mariposa, mmaaa riposa, comienza con /ma/?" Si, entonces redondeamos mariposa. ¿Qué es? sí, montaña mmmooontaña, comienza con /ma/? No. Pasemos al dibujo siguiente. ¿Qué es? Sí, mapa, mmmaaapa, comienza con /ma/?" Sí, entonces redondear mapa. ¿Qué es? Sí, medusa. Mmmeee dusa, empieza con mmmaaa? No, entonces no la redondeamos.

Do:

You read the syllable "ma". You point to the first picture and say the name of the picture, stretching the first Syllable sound. You proceed with the rest of the pictures.

 **Aprendo a leer y escribir**

IMPLEMENTATION: **LESSON SAMPLES**

> **PRACTICE TIP:**
> - In this activity you can choose to color or circle the correct picture, depending on how much time she wants to spend with this activity.

Activity #10

The student names the picture, identifies the first syllable, and writes it down.

 Say:

Escribe la sílaba inicial para cada dibujo. ¿Qué es? Sí, es mamá, mmmaaamá, ¿con qué sílaba empieza, (pause) /ma.../ sí, con /ma/, ahora escribimos /ma/, ¿cuál es la primera letra de la sílaba /ma?? /m/ y la que sigue? /a/ ¿qué dice? .../ma/

Do:

You point to "mother" and ask the student to say its name slowly and to identify that first syllable. Then show the student the lines where to write the syllable.

> **PRACTICE TIP:**
> - If the student struggles with this isolating that first syllable, use a materialization technique for syllable awareness from this guide.

Activity #11

Categorization; student sorts pictures by its initial syllable sound.

 Say:

Recorta los dibujos y pégalos en la siguiente página según su sílaba inicial.

Do:

You ask the students to cut and then paste the pictures under the correct syllable.

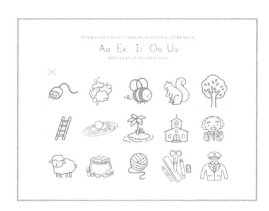

IMPLEMENTATION: **LESSON SAMPLES**

Aprendo a leer y escribir

Activity #12

Game. Students practice reading the syllables fluently.

Say:

"Necesitas un amigo y un dado. Tira los dados y colorea el número de burbujas que indiquen los dados. Lee las sílabas de las burbujas que coloreas. Gana el que coloreo más burbujas."

Do:

Students play the game in pairs. They throw a dice and color the bubbles that the dice show.

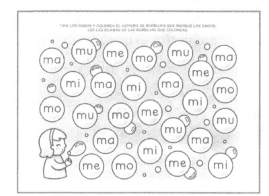

PRACTICE TIP:

- You can ask the students to say words that begin with all the different syllables while coloring them, for vocabulary practice.

In Aprendo a leer y escribir workbooks #1 to #5, activities are sequenced following the same pattern. After completion of activities #1 to #12 for each syllable introduced, there are four more activities, #13 to #16, where each new syllable is combined with the previous ones to make new words. Here are lesson plan samples for activities #13 to #16 for syllables ma, me, mi, mo, mu and pa, pe, pi, po, pu combined.

Activity #13

The student reads two words and selects the one that matches the picture. (pg. 27)

Say:

Lee las palabras que están debajo del dibujo. Redondea la palabra que corresponde al dibujo. ¿Qué dice aquí? ¿Y aquí? ¿Qué palabra debes redondear?

II - 26

Aprendo a leer y escribir

IMPLEMENTATION: **LESSON SAMPLES**

Do:

You point to words and ask the student to read the words. Try to make them read both of the word options for each picture to practice reading.

Activity #14

In this activity the students need to read and blend syllables to make the word that matches the picture. (pg. 28)

Say:

Conecta con una línea las sílabas para formar la palabra. ¿Qué es? Si, un mapa. Acá dice ma… po? ma…pu? ma…pa? Sí acá dice ma… pa.
Entonces conectamos /ma/ con /pa/ con una línea.

Do:

You point to the picture, ask students what it is. Then you read the first syllable with each of the possible second syllables. Students decide which syllables make the word that matches the picture.

Activity #15

The student fills in boxes with the missing letters to make a word that matches a picture. (pg 29)

Say:

Completa la palabra con las letras que faltan. ¿Qué es? Si, mamá. /m…m…/ ¿qué letras debemos escribir para que diga mamá? y aquí dice /a…a/. ¿Qué letras van en estas cajitas? y aquí… ¿Qué letras van?

Do:

You point to the picture and ask the students to fill in the boxes with the missing letters.

IMPLEMENTATION: **LESSON SAMPLES**

Activity #16

Students need to sequence the letters correctly to make a word. (pg.30)

Say:

"Ordena las letras para formar la palabra".
"Leamos las palabras en las cajitas, para saber qué palabras pueden ir en los vagones del tren".
"Ahora leamos las letras en las nubes del primer tren: /m/m/a/a/, ¿Qué palabra podemos formar con esas letras? Recuerden que es una palabra de las que leímos en las cajitas".

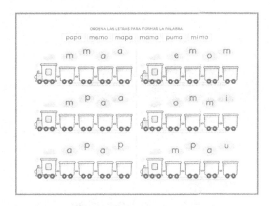

Do:

You point to the word boxes on the top of the page and ask the student to read them all. Then you ask the student to read the letters inside the clouds. Ask the students to make one of the words that is in the word boxes.

> You continue using the same script as for the syllable "ma, me, mi, mo, mu" with the rest of the syllables.

SECTION III

SUPPLEMENTAL ACTIVITIES

1. Syllable Awareness Technique
2. Syllable Segmentation
3. Phoneme Segmentation
4. Syllable Blending
5. Phoneme Blending
6. Guided Word Building
7. Spelling

Teaching Guide
Phonetic Syllabic Method

Supplemental Activities

The following section includes activities that you can use with Aprendo a leer y escribir to enhance and strengthen specific skills depending on a student's specific needs. The supplemental activities include phonological awareness development through materialization techniques, word formation activities, and spelling exercises. You can use these exercises selectively and in a flexible manner in 5-10 minute sessions to enhance a lesson.

Phonological Awareness and Materialization Techniques

To become readers and writers, students "must acquire a sense of the correspondence between letters and sounds". This is what Marylyn Adams (1) calls the "Alphabetic Principle". Phonological awareness is the essential skill students need to develop to be able to establish that one on one correspondence between letters and sounds.

The following activities leverage materialization techniques to help students develop phonological awareness (syllabic and phonemic awareness). Through these activities, students learn to develop orally what they later learn to do with the written word. They learn to hear, identify, and manipulate sounds in spoken words.

Materialization techniques as defined by J. Richard Gentry (2) use tangible objects or physical processes to help students establish and reinforce an abstract concept, in this case, the relationship between letters and sounds. The materialization techniques included in this guide are designed to help students represent the sounds in a word.

While there are many activities that can help students develop phonological awareness, research shows that "phonemic awareness instruction is most effective when it focuses on only one or two types of phoneme manipulation, rather than several types"(3). The phonological awareness practice activities included in this guide focus on syllable and phoneme segmentation and syllable and phoneme blending.

(1) Marilyn Jager Adams, (1990). *Beginning to read: Thinking and Learning about Print.* Cambridge, MA: MIT Press.
(2) J. Richard Gentry, Ph.D, (2006). *Breaking the Code: The New Science of Beginning Reading and Writing.* Portsmouth, NH: Heinemann.
(3) Bonnie B. Ambruster, Ph.D, Fran Lehr, Jean Osborn,M Ed, (2001). *Put Reading First: The Research Building Blocks for Teaching Children to Read.* National Institute for Literacy at ED Pubs.

SYLLABLE AWARENESS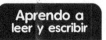

```
        MATERIALIZATION TECHNIQUES
                    ↓
     PHONOLOGICAL AWARENESS DEVELOPMENT
                    ↓
            ALPHABETIC PRINCIPLE
                    ↓
            READING AND WRITING
```

Exercises to Develop Word Segmenting and Word Blending Skills

1. Syllable Awareness Techniques

In order to become proficient readers, students need to become aware of syllables in words. They need to learn to identify and recognize a syllable in a word. The following exercise provides a simple and effective way to make students notice the individual syllables in a word.

Say:

"La sílaba es un grupo de letras que se pronuncian con una sola emisión de voz. Para reconocer sílabas en una palabra, colocamos la mano debajo del mentón, presten atención que ocurre con nuestra boca cuando decimos una palabra, por ejemplo "mano"... ¿qué ocurrió? Abrimos la boca dos veces, cuando dijimos /ma/ y otra vez cuando dijimos /no/. Cada vez que abrimos la boca, es porque estamos diciendo una sílaba, una parte pequeña de la palabra que siempre tiene una vocal incluída."

Do:

Ask the students to place their hand under the chin, then ask them to say a word, and encourage them to notice every time their jaw moves. Every movement of the jaw is a syllable.

SYLLABLE SEGMENTATION

> ## PRACTICE TIPS
> ### FOR ALL OF THE FOLLOWING ACTIVITIES
>
> - For best results, repeat each of the following activities with **4 to 6 words** for reinforcement.
>
> - Each time you invite a student to practice a new activity with a word, **ask the student to repeat the word after you say it.** That way, you'll be sure that the student heard the word correctly.

2. Syllable Segmentation

Students break a word into its separate syllable sounds.

2.1. Clapping out Syllables

Say:

"La sílaba son las pequeñas partes que forman una palabra. Vamos a practicar reconocer sílabas, palmeando (o golpeando con la mano en la mesa para cada sílaba que escuchamos) cada vez que escuchamos una sílaba. Vamos a ver cuántas partes tiene la palabra "mano" /ma/ /no/, dos, muy bien."

Do:

Students clap hands for each syllable when they say a word aloud. Start out by modeling the activity until the students can clap out the syllables in words they are in the process of learning from the book Aprendo a leer y escribir. Count the syllables while clapping or tapping. Once you choose a mode, stay with it.

> **PRACTICE TIP:**
> - Use words from activity #14 in **Aprendo a leer y escribir** from the target syllable.

PHONEME SEGMENTATION

2.2. Written Words Syllable Division

Students break up a written word into its separate syllable sounds,.

Say:

"Leamos juntos esta palabra "mesa". ¿Cuántas sílabas tiene "mesa"? /me/ /sa/ sí, dos. Tracemos una línea para separar cada sílaba (o tracemos una línea curva debajo de cada sílaba)"

Do:

Write a word on the whiteboard, for example, "mesa", and ask the student to divide the word in syllables by drawing a line in between the two syllables or under it.

3. Phoneme Segmentation

Students break a word into its separate phoneme sounds. The following four activities practice this task.

3.1. Stretching out the Sounds in Words

This exercise makes use of any stretchable fabric (elastic band) to help students become aware of each individual sound in a word through visualization and physical sensation.

Say:

"Vamos a escuchar los sonidos que forman la palabra "mono", /mmm//ooo//nnn//ooo//mono/"

Do:

Ask students to hold an elastic band in front of themselves at the reading level and to stretch out the band as you and your students pronounces the word very slowly, exaggerating each phoneme until the band is fully extended. Then allow the band to go back to the original position and say the word all at once.

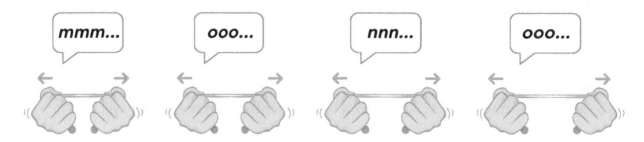

PHONEME SEGMENTATION

3.2. Finger Spelling

This materialization technique designates the number of phonemes in a word thereby helping students identify each phoneme. Students who learn finger spelling successfully have full phonemic awareness.

"Mono. ¿Cuál es el primer sonido? /m/ lo ponemos en el dedo pulgar (hold up the thumb) ¿cuál es el sonido siguiente? /o/ lo ponemos en el dedo índice (hold up the index finger) ¿cuál es el sonido siguiente? /n/ lo ponemos en el dedo mayor o en este dedo (hold up middle finger) ¿cuál es el sonido final? /o/ lo ponemos en el dedo anular o este dedo (hold up pinky finger). ¿Cuántas letras tiene mono? Contemos los dedos... cuatro."

To fingerspell the word "mono" put each sound on a finger by holding a finger up each time the sound is said starting with the thumb.

PRACTICE TIP:
- Avoid naming fingers by their common name to not overload students with information.

3.3. Finger Tapping for Segmentation

Finger tapping is a segmenting technique that helps students hear the individual sounds in a word.

"Vamos a tocar cada dedo con el pulgar para cada uno de los sonidos en la palabra "mono". /m/ /o/ /n/ /o/

Students tap different fingers to their thumb for each sound they hear in a word.

SYLLABLE BLENDING

Aprendo a leer y escribir

m

- Tap your index (dedo índice) finger with your thumb and say /m/.

o

- Then tap your middle (dedo del medio) finger with your thumb and say /o/.

n

- Then tap your ring (dedo anular) finger with your thumb and say /n/.

o

- Finally tap your pinky (dedo meñique o pequeño) finger with your thumb and says /o/.

PRACTICE TIP:
Start by modeling the activity with a few words, then do it together with the students until they are able to tap words independently.

PHONEME BLENDING

3.4. Elkonin Boxes

Elkonin Boxes make use of a materialization technique that builds phonological awareness through the segmentation of words into individual sounds. The technique is named after **D.B. Elkonin**, the Russian psychologist who pioneered its use.

Say:

"Ahora vamos a mirar una imagen, decir que es, por ejemplo "mano" y escuchar los sonidos de la palabra "mano". Vamos a poner una gema/ficha en un cuadrado cada vez que escuchemos un sonido. Comencemos con la palabra mano primero. ¿Qué ves? "Mano", correcto. Entonces, cuando decimos la palabra "mano" y la separamos en sus sonidos, suena así: /mmm/ /aaa/ /nnnn/ /ooo/ Puedo poner una gema aquí para /m/ y una gema aquí para /a/, otra aquí para /n/ y otra aquí para /o/. (Decimos los sonidos mientras ponemos las fichas/gemas dentro de los cuadrados (o cajitas)."

Do:

- Print and cut out the Elkonin boxes. Laminate the boxes for durability if desired. You can also just draw the squares on a piece of paper or a whiteboard. Use small objects that are fun to manipulate, for example, chips or colorful glass gems.

- Place a card in front of the student. Start with a simple one that has only two boxes and practice with isolated syllables first.

- Slide the tokens one by one into the boxes while saying each sound).

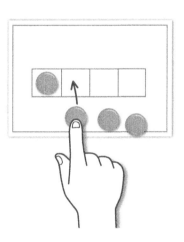

4. Syllable Blending

Students listen to two syllables in isolation and then they combine them to make a word.

4.1. Syllable Blending

It is recommended to start blending syllables and then phonemes since the syllable as a unit of sound is easier to reproduce than the phoneme in isolation.

Say:

*"Voy a decir una palabra muy despacio sílaba por sílaba. Luego diré las sílabas un poco más rápido. "¿Qué palabra es /mmmaaa/..." (pause for 2 seconds) "/nnnnooooo/, ¿todo junto? "mano".
Ahora diré otro ejemplo (maestro dice sílabas mas rápido) /mo//no/, ¿todo junto? /mono/"*

PHONEME BLENDING

Do:

The children have to orally blend the word parts and say the words as a whole.

> **PRACTICE TIPS:**
> - You can do this orally, and you can use a puppet to make it more fun. Explain that the puppet only likes to say whole words.
> - Another option is a materialization technique that uses your hands. Put a syllable on your fist and another syllable on your other fist and then move the two fists together while saying the whole word.

4.2. Syllable - Phoneme Blending

In this exercise, students blend a single syllable with two phonemes. This is a transition to phoneme blending, where students hear phonemes in isolation and then combine them into a word.

Say:

"*Voy a decir una palabra despacio en partes y después la diré más rapido toda junta: /me/ /s/ /a/, toda junta /mesa/*".

Do:

Students listen separately to a spoken syllable and two phonemes and then combine them to form a word.

5. Phoneme Blending

5.1. Oral Phoneme Blending

In this activity, students are asked to create a word out of discrete phonemes.

Say:

"*Voy a decir los sonidos que forman una palabra y después diré la palabra toda junta: /m/ /u/ /l/ /a/, toda junta /mula/. (otra opción: "¿Qué palabra es /m/ /a/ /n/ /o/?")*"

Do:

Students listen separately four phonemes and then they combine them to form a word.

GUIDED WORD BUILDING

> **PRACTICE TIPS:**
> Phoneme blending is the most difficult of the three blending tasks described above. Return to an easier task if you notice that students are struggling.
> • A variation of this activity, it can be to use the fingerspelling materialization technique. You put a letter in each finger and then you close and open all the fingers saying the whole word.

5.2. Finger Tapping for Blending

Finger tapping is a technique that helps students learn how to blend phonemes.

"Ustedes hagan lo mismo que yo. /m/ (en dedo índice) /o/ (dedo del medio) /n/ (en dedo anular) /o/ (en dedo meñique). Ahora decimos la palabra juntando todos los sonidos /mono/."

You model the activity first. Students tap different fingers to their thumb for each sound you tell them to. Students blend the sounds and say the word, while dragging their thumb across the fingers, starting with their index finger.

6. Guided Word Building

Guided word building is a guide to hands-on Phonics in which students make words from letter tiles. Students will need a full set of letter tiles for these activities. You may use magnetic, plastic, or paper tiles.

In a classroom setting, you might use an overhead projector to build the same word the students are building at their seats. That way they can check their work. A pocket chart can also be used. Be sure students have all the letter tiles they will need for the current lesson.

There are two different approaches to guided word building, one emphasizing spelling, the other reading. Choose the approach you want to use depending on the skill you want to practice at any given time.

6.1. Making Words for Spelling Practice

In this activity students spell words using tiles. This exercise helps students develop their encoding skills (spelling). Students manipulate letters to make words.

GUIDED WORD BUILDING

Say:

"Vamos a escribir la palabra "pato". Toma las letras que necesites para escribir la palabra pato. Ponlas en el orden correcto para que diga "pato."

Do:

When students are ready, say a word out loud. Ask students to build the word by selecting the appropiate letter tiles and placing them in the correct order.

> **PRACTICE TIPS:**
>
> This activity can be done with varying degrees of difficulty.
> - Easy: Provide the students just with the letter tiles they need to make a certain word. In this variant, the student needs to focus only on the sequencing of the letters.
> - More difficult: Give students all the letter tiles for the entire alphabet. The student must decide which letters are needed to make the word.

6.2. Making Words for Reading Practice

This activity helps students develop their decoding skills (reading). In this activity you make the word and the student reads it.

Say:

"Voy a formar una palabra, luego tú vas a leer la palabra. (Maestro forma "pala")" ¿Puedes leer esta palabra?"

Do:

You choose a word, you pick the letters and make the word. Then you ask the student to read it.

> **PRACTICE TIPS:**
>
> • If the student cannot read the word, separate the word in syllables and then ask the student to read the syllables first and then the whole word together.
>
> • A variation in this activity can be telling the student the letters needed to make the word. Then tell the student the letters in the correct sequence so that the student builds the word by putting them in the correct order. Finally, ask the student to read the word out loud.

GUIDED WORD BUILDING

6.3. Making Words for Reading with Letter Substitution

In this activity students read words where discrete phonemes are substitute by others.

Say:

"Esta palabra dice "pala" ahora vamos a cambiar la letra /a/ por esta letra (maestro cambia la "a" por la "o" pero no pronuncia la letra "o") ¿Qué palabra formamos ahora? Muy bien "palo". Y ahora cambiemos esta letra (maestra quita la "l" y coloca una "t" en su lugar) ¿Qué palabra formamos ahora? Muy bien "pato".

Do:

You make a word, your read it and then switch one of the letters. You ask the student to read the new word.

> **PRACTICE TIPS:**
> - Continue changing letters and asking the students to read the new words.
> - Vary the exercise by asking the student to switch one letter for another one and then ask the student to read the word.
>
> **Say:**
>
> "Esta palabra dice "sopa" ahora cambia la letra "s" (maestro puede usar el sonido o nombre de letra) por la letra "r". ¿Puedes leer esta palabra ahora?"

Extension Activity for Word Building Practice

In this activity, each word that students builds is copied on an index card. When the word-making session is over, students read the words from their index cards and save them in a word box. These word banks can be used for later, for reading and writing activities.

Some examples are:
- Just practice reading the words.
- Practice spelling this word: copying or write the words from dictation on a whiteboard or paper.
- Choose words from the word box and ask students to use them in a sentence.
- Sort the words by beginning syllable.

6.4. Making Syllables for Spelling Practice

This activity helps students develop their encoding skills for Syllables (spelling). Students make syllables with tiles.

SPELLING

> **Say:**
>
> *"Vamos a escribir la sílaba "le". Toma las letras que necesites para escribir la sílaba "le". Ponlas en el orden correcto para que diga "le". Ahora la sílaba "la".*
> *¿Qué hiciste para que diga "la"? Ahora escribe "lo"..."lu"...."li"..."*

> **Do:**
>
> Ask students to build syllables by selecting the appropriate letters and placing them in the correct order. You can ask students to practice syllables with same consonant and changing the vowel, or keep the same vowel and vary the consonant.

6.5. Making Syllables for Reading Practice

This activity helps students develop their decoding skills (reading). In this activity, you make the syllable and the student reads it.

> **Say:**
>
> *"Voy a formar una sílaba, luego tú vas a leerla. (maestro forma "se") "¿Puedes leer esta sílaba?" (maestro forma "so") ¿Y ahora qué dice? (maestro forma "su") ¿Y ahora...?"*

> **Do:**
>
> You choose a syllable, you pick the letters and build it. Then you ask the student to read the word out loud. You can either vary the vowels or the consonants.

> **PRACTICE TIPS:**
> Making syllables is a good reading practice for students who struggle to recall how to read syllables.

7. Spelling

7.1. Spelling Syllables

Students spell syllables from dictation after practicing making syllables with letters tiles.

> **Say:**
>
> *"Vamos a escribir sílabas en la pizarra (o papel). Escriban "lu", "la", etc."*

> **Do:**
>
> You dictate target syllables. You can dictate them following the order "a, e, i, o, u" or in a random order.

SPELLING

7.2. Spelling Words

Students spell words from dictation. After practicing with materialization techniques and having done word building activities, students may be ready to spell words without errors.

"Vamos a escribir en la pizarra (o papel) las palabras que ya practicamos con las letras móviles (magnéticas). Escriban la palabra "sapo", ahora escriban "sopa".

You dictate words already practiced in previous activities.

> **PRACTICE TIPS:**
>
> You can choose words that differ in one or two letters only. For example: "pato, palo, pala" That way students need to focus on what is different from one word to another. This type of practice helps develop phonemic awareness.

7.3. Share Spelling

Share spelling means that the student shares the spelling of a word with the teacher through proper scaffolding. This activity is useful for students who haven't yet established the one on one correspondence between letters and sounds.

"Vamos a escribir la palabra "luna". Díme que sonidos escuchas cuando decimos /luna/ (estudiante dice /u/ /a/) muy bien escribimos la /u/ sobre esta línea y la /a/ sobre esta línea. ¿Qué otro sonido escuchas, /l l l/ lu/ sí /l/ muy bien, la /l/ es la primer letra. Acá dice /lua/. Queremos que diga /lunnna/ ¿qué más escuchas, muy bien la /n/ que va en este espacio. Lee tu la palabra."

Do:

- Draw a line for each letter of the word to be spelled (like in the game hangman.)
- Say the word to be spelled out loud and ask the student to repeat the word.
- Ask the student to say what letters he or she hears that make up the word. The student replies and you write down on the lines the letters (only the correct ones) provided by the student.
- Help the student with the missing letters or with letter sequencing, as needed.

SECTION IV

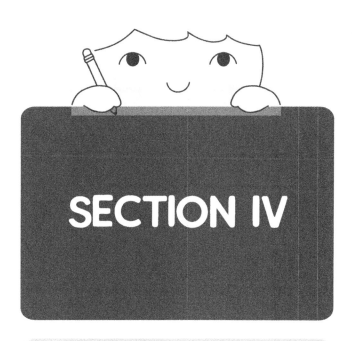

UNIT'S LEARNING PLAN

1. Scope for INTENSIVE Instruction
2. Scope for READING INTERVENTION Instruction
3. Scope for AT GRADE LEVEL Instruction
4. Scope for ACCELERATED Instruction

Teaching Guide
Phonetic Syllabic Method

Aprendo a leer y escribir

SCOPE FOR

INTENSIVE INSTRUCTION

• UNIT 1 (book 1)

Week 1   **LESSON 1:** Letter **Aa** (20 minutes 3 x per week)

DAY 1
- Activity # 1
- Activity # 2*
  *additional tracing practice

DAY 2
- Activity # 3
- Activity # 4

DAY 3
- Activity # 5
- Activity # 6

Week 2   **LESSON 2:** Letter **Ee** (20 minutes 3 x per week)

DAY 1
- Activity # 1
- Activity # 2*
  *additional tracing practice

DAY 2
- Activity # 3
- Activity # 4

DAY 3
- Activity # 5
- Activity # 6
- A-E Activity

Week 3   **LESSON 3:** Letter **Ii** (20 minutes 3 x per week)

DAY 1
- Activity # 1
- Activity # 2*
  *additional tracing practice

DAY 2
- Activity # 3
- Activity # 4

DAY 3
- Activity # 5
- Activity # 6
- A-E-I Activity

Week 4   **LESSON 4:** Letter **Oo** (20 minutes 3 x per week)

DAY 1
- Activity # 1
- Activity # 2*
  *additional tracing practice

DAY 2
- Activity # 3
- Activity # 4

DAY 3
- Activity # 5
- Activity # 6
- A-E-I-O Activity

IV - 47

SCOPE FOR INTENSIVE INSTRUCTION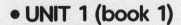

• UNIT 1 (book 1)

Week 5 — **LESSON 5:** Letter **Uu** (20 minutes 3 x per week)

DAY 1	DAY 2	DAY 3
• Activity # 1 • Activity # 2* *additional tracing practice	• Activity # 3 • Activity # 4	• Activity # 5 • Activity # 6

Week 6 — **LESSON 6:** Review **Vowels**

DAY 1	DAY 2	DAY 3
• A-E-I-O-U Activity • Activity # 10	• Activity # 13 • Activity # 12	• Activity # 11 • Supplemental activities (see section II of this guide) • Card games with 5 vowels: Go fish, Memory (you can use uppercase and lowercase tiles/cards)

• UNIT 2 (book 2)

Week 1 — **LESSON 1:** Syllables **ma, me, mi, mo, mu** (20 minutes 4 x per week)

DAY 1	DAY 2	DAY 3	DAY 4
• Activity # 1 • Activity # 2 • Activity # 3 • Activity # 4 • Supplemental Activities	• Activity # 5 • Activity # 6 • Activity # 7 • Activity # 8 • Supplemental Activities • Game: Syllables Memory	• Activity # 9 • Activity # 10 • Activity # 11 • Activity # 12 • Supplemental Activities	• Activity # 13 • Activity # 14 • Activity # 15 • Activity # 16 • Supplemental Activities

SCOPE FOR
 INTENSIVE INSTRUCTION

• UNIT 2 (book 2)

Week 2 — **LESSON 2:** Syllables **pa, pe, pi, po, pu** (20 minutes 4 x per week)
You follow the same teaching plan as in week 1, of Unit 2.

Week 3 — **LESSON 3:** Syllables **sa, se, si, so, su** (20 minutes 4 x per week)
You follow the same teaching plan as in week 1, of Unit 2.

Week 4 — **LESSON 4:** Syllables **ta, te, ti, to, tu** (20 minutes 4 x per week)
You follow the same teaching plan as in week 1, of Unit 2.

Week 5 — **LESSON 5:** Syllables **la, le, li, lo, lu** (20 minutes 4 x per week)
You follow the same teaching plan as in week 1, of Unit 2.

• UNIT 3 (book 3)

Week 1 — **LESSON 1:** Syllables **ra, re, ri, ro, ru** (20 minutes 4 x per week)
You follow the same teaching plan as in week 1, of Unit 2.

Week 2 — **LESSON 2:** Syllables **na, ne, ni, no, nu** (20 minutes 4 x per week)
You follow the same teaching plan as in week 1, of Unit 2.

Week 3 — **LESSON 3:** Syllables **ba, be, bi, bo, bu** (20 minutes 4 x per week)
You follow the same teaching plan as in week 1, of Unit 2.

Week 4 — **LESSON 4:** Syllables **fa, fe, fi, fo, fu** (20 minutes 4 x per week)
You follow the same teaching plan as in week 1, of Unit 2.

SCOPE FOR INTENSIVE INSTRUCTION

• UNIT 3 (book 3)

Week 5 — **LESSON 5:** Syllables **da, de, di, do, du** (20 minutes 4 x per week)

You follow the same teaching plan as in week 1, of Unit 2.

• UNIT 4 (book 4)

Week 1 — **LESSON 1:** Syllables **ca, co, cu** (20 minutes 4 x per week)

You follow the same teaching plan as in week 1, of Unit 2.

Week 2 — **LESSON 2:** Syllables **ce, ci, que, qui** (20 minutes 4 x per week)

DAY 1	DAY 2	DAY 3	DAY 4
• Activity # 1 (ce, ci)	• Activity # 4	• Activity # 8	• Activity # 13
• Activity # 1 (que, qui)	• Activity # 5	• Activity # 9	• Activity # 14
• Activity # 2	• Activity # 6	• Activity # 10	• Activity # 15
• Activity # 3 (ce, ci)	• Activity # 7	• Activity # 11	• Activity # 16
• Activity # 3 (que, qui)	• Supplemental Activities	• Activity # 12	• Supplemental Activities
		• Supplemental Activities	

Week 3 — **LESSON 3:** Syllables **ja, je, ji, jo, ju** (20 minutes 4 x per week)

You follow the same teaching plan as in week 1, of Unit 2.

Week 4 — **LESSON 4:** Syllables **ga, go, gu** (20 minutes 4 x per week)

You follow the same teaching plan as in week 1, of Unit 2.

SCOPE FOR INTENSIVE INSTRUCTION

• UNIT 4 (book 4)

Week 5 — LESSON 5: Syllables **ge, gi, gue, gui** (20 minutes 4 x per week)

DAY 1	DAY 2	DAY 3	DAY 4
• Activity # 1 (ge, gi) • Activity # 1 (gue, gui) • Activity # 3 (ge, gi) • Activity # 3 (gue, gui) • Activity # 4 • Supplemental Activities	• Activity # 5 • Activity # 6 • Activity # 7 • Supplemental Activities	• Activity # 8 • Activity # 9 • Activity # 10 • Activity # 11 • Activity # 12 • Supplemental Activities	• Activity # 13 • Activity # 14 • Activity # 15 • Activity # 16 • Supplemental Activities

Week 6 — LESSON 6: Syllables **cha, che, chi, cho, chu** (20 minutes 4 x per week)

You follow the same teaching plan as in week 1, of Unit 2.

• UNIT 5 (book 5)

Week 1 — LESSON 1: Syllables **va, ve, vi, vo, vu** (20 minutes 4 x per week)

You follow the same teaching plan as in week 1, of Unit 2.

Week 2 — LESSON 2: Syllables **lla, lle, lli, llo, llu** (20 minutes 4 x per week)

You follow the same teaching plan as in week 1, of Unit 2.

Week 3 — LESSON 3: Syllables **ya, ye, yi, yo, yu** (20 minutes 4 x per week)

You follow the same teaching plan as in week 1, of Unit 2.

SCOPE FOR INTENSIVE INSTRUCTION

Aprendo a leer y escribir

• UNIT 5 (book 5)

Week 4 — **LESSON 4:** Syllables **za, ze, zi, zo, zu** (20 minutes 4 x per week)

You follow the same teaching plan as in week 1, of Unit 2.

Week 5 — **LESSON 5:** Syllables **ha, he, hi, ho, hu** (20 minutes 4 x per week)

You follow the same teaching plan as in week 1, of Unit 2.

Week 6 — **LESSON 6:** Syllables **ki, ko, wa, wi** (20 minutes 4 x per week)

DAY 1
- Activity # 1
- Activity # 2 (letter formation K)
- Activity # 2 (letter formation W)
- Activity # 3
- Activity # 4
- Supplemental Activities

DAY 2
- Activity # 5
- Activity # 6
- Activity # 7
- Supplemental Activities

DAY 3
- Activity # 8
- Activity # 9
- Activity # 10
- Activity # 11
- Activity # 12 (game syllables with K)
- Activity # 12 (game syllables with W)
- Supplemental Activities

Week 7 — **LESSON 7:** Syllables **xi, ña, ño** (20 minutes 4 x per week)

DAY 1
- Activity # 1
- Activity # 2 (letter formation X)
- Activity # 2 (letter formation Ñ)
- Activity # 5
- Activity # 6
- Supplemental Activities

DAY 2
- Activity # 7
- Activity # 8, # 10
- Activity # 12 (game syllables with X)
- Activity # 12 (game syllables with Ñ)
- Supplemental Activities

Aprendo a leer y escribir

SCOPE FOR READING INTERVENTION INSTRUCTION

• UNIT 1 (book 1)

Week 1

LESSON 1:
Letter **Aa** (10/20 minutes 4 x per week)

DAY 1
- Activity # 1
- Activity # 2
- Activity # 3

DAY 2
- Activity # 4
- Activity # 5
- Activity # 6

LESSON 2:
Letter **Ee** (10/20 minutes 4 x per week)

DAY 3
- Activity # 1
- Activity # 2
- Activity # 3

DAY 4
- Activity # 4
- Activity # 5
- Activity # 6
- A-E Activity

Week 2

LESSON 3:
Letter **Ii** (10/20 minutes 4 x per week)

DAY 1
- Activity # 1
- Activity # 2
- Activity # 3

DAY 2
- Activity # 4
- Activity # 5
- Activity # 6
- A-E-I Activity

LESSON 4:
Letter **Oo** (10/20 minutes 4 x per week)

DAY 3
- Activity # 1
- Activity # 2
- Activity # 3

DAY 4
- Activity # 4
- Activity # 5
- Activity # 6
- A-E-I-O Activity

Week 3   LESSON 5: Letter **Uu** (20 minutes 3 x per week)

DAY 1
- Activity # 1
- Activity # 2
- Activity # 3

DAY 2
- Activity # 4
- Activity # 5
- Activity # 6

DAY 3
- A-E-I-O-U Activity
- Activity # 10
- Activity # 13

DAY 4
- Activity # 11
- Activity # 12

IV - 53

SCOPE FOR READING INTERVENTION INSTRUCTION

Aprendo a leer y escribir

• UNIT 2 (book 2)

Week 1 — LESSON 1: Syllables **ma, me, mi, mo, mu** (10/20 minutes 4 x per week)

DAY 1	DAY 2	DAY 3	DAY 4
• Activity # 1 • Activity # 2 • Activity # 3 • Activity # 4 • Supplemental Activities	• Activity # 5 • Activity # 6 • Activity # 7 • Activity # 8 • Supplemental Activities • Game: Syllables Memory	• Activity # 9 • Activity # 10 • Activity # 11 • Activity # 12 • Supplemental Activities	• Activity # 13 • Activity # 14 • Activity # 15 • Activity # 16 • Supplemental Activities

Week 2 — LESSON 2: Syllables **pa, pe, pi, po, pu** (10/20 minutes 4 x per week)

You follow the same teaching plan as in week 1, of Unit 2.

Week 3 — LESSON 3: Syllables **sa, se, si, so, su** (10/20 minutes 4 x per week)

You follow the same teaching plan as in week 1, of Unit 2.

Week 4 — LESSON 4: Syllables **ta, te, ti, to, tu** (10/20 minutes 4 x per week)

You follow the same teaching plan as in week 1, of Unit 2.

Week 5 — LESSON 5: Syllables **la, le, li, lo, lu** (10/20 minutes 4 x per week)

You follow the same teaching plan as in week 1, of Unit 2.

• UNIT 3 (book 3)

Week 1 — LESSON 1: Syllables **ra, re, ri, ro, ru** (10/20 minutes 4 x per week)

You follow the same teaching plan as in week 1, of Unit 2.

SCOPE FOR
READING INTERVENTION INSTRUCTION

• UNIT 3 (book 3)

Week 2 — **LESSON 2:** Syllables **na, ne, ni, no, nu** (10/20 minutes 4 x per week)
You follow the same teaching plan as in week 1, of Unit 2.

Week 3 — **LESSON 3:** Syllables **ba, be, bi, bo, bu** (10/20 minutes 4 x per week)
You follow the same teaching plan as in week 1, of Unit 2.

Week 4 — **LESSON 4:** Syllables **fa, fe, fi, fo, fu** (10/20 minutes 4 x per week)
You follow the same teaching plan as in week 1, of Unit 2.

Week 5 — **LESSON 5:** Syllables **da, de, di, do, du** (10/20 minutes 4 x per week)
You follow the same teaching plan as in week 1, of Unit 2.

• UNIT 4 (book 4)

Week 1 — **LESSON 1:** Syllables **ca, co, cu** (10/20 minutes 4 x per week)
You follow the same teaching plan as in week 1, of Unit 2.

Week 2 — **LESSON 2:** Syllables **ce, ci, que, qui** (10/20 minutes 4 x per week)

DAY 1	DAY 2	DAY 3	DAY 4
• Activity # 1 (ce, ci) • Activity # 1 (que, qui) • Activity # 2 • Activity # 3 (ce, ci) • Activity # 3 (que, qui)	• Supplemental Activities • Activity # 4 • Activity # 5 • Activity # 6 • Activity # 7 • Supplemental Activities • Game: Syllables Memory	• Activity # 8 • Activity # 9 • Activity # 10 • Activity # 11 • Activity # 12 • Supplemental Activities	• Activity # 13 • Activity # 14 • Activity # 15 • Activity # 16 • Supplemental Activities

SCOPE FOR READING INTERVENTION INSTRUCTION

• UNIT 4 (book 4)

Week 3 — **LESSON 3:** Syllables **ja, je, ji, jo, ju** (10/20 minutes 4 x per week)
You follow the same teaching plan as in week 1, of Unit 2.

Week 4 — **LESSON 4:** Syllables **ga, go, gu** (10/20 minutes 4 x per week)
You follow the same teaching plan as in week 1, of Unit 2.

Week 5 — **LESSON 5:** Syllables **ge, gi, gue, gui** (10/20 minutes 4 x per week)

DAY 1	DAY 2	DAY 3	DAY 4
• Activity # 1 (ge, gi)	• Activity # 5	• Activity # 8	• Activity # 13
• Activity # 1 (gue, gui)	• Activity # 6	• Activity # 9	• Activity # 14
• Activity # 3 (ge, gi)	• Activity # 7	• Activity # 10	• Activity # 15
• Activity # 3 (gue, gui)	• Supplemental Activities	• Activity # 11	• Activity # 16
• Activity # 4	• Game: Syllables Memory	• Activity # 12	• Supplemental Activities
• Supplemental Activities		• Supplemental Activities	

Week 6 — **LESSON 6:** Syllables **cha, che, chi, cho, chu** (10/20 minutes 4 x per week)
You follow the same teaching plan as in week 1, of Unit 2.

• UNIT 5 (book 5)

Week 1 — **LESSON 1:** Syllables **va, ve, vi, vo, vu** (10/20 minutes 4 x per week)
You follow the same teaching plan as in week 1, of Unit 2.

• UNIT 5 (book 5)

Week 2 — **LESSON 2:** Syllables **lla, lle, lli, llo, llu** (10/20 minutes 4 x per week)
You follow the same teaching plan as in week 1, of Unit 2.

Week 3 — **LESSON 3:** Syllables **ya, ye, yi, yo, yu** (10/20 minutes 4 x per week)
You follow the same teaching plan as in week 1, of Unit 2.

Week 4 — **LESSON 4:** Syllables **za, ze, zi, zo, zu** (10/20 minutes 4 x per week)
You follow the same teaching plan as in week 1, of Unit 2.

Week 5 — **LESSON 5:** Syllables **ha, he, hi, ho, hu** (10/20 minutes 4 x per week)
You follow the same teaching plan as in week 1, of Unit 2.

Week 6 — **LESSON 6:** Syllables **ki, ko, wa, wi** (10/20 minutes 4 x per week)

DAY 1
- Activity # 1
- Activity # 2 (letter formation K)
- Activity # 2 (letter formation W)
- Activity # 3
- Activity # 4
- Supplemental Activities

DAY 2
- Activity # 5
- Activity # 6
- Activity # 7
- Supplemental Activities
- Game: Syllables Memory

DAY 3
- Activity # 8
- Activity # 9
- Activity # 10
- Activity # 11
- Activity # 12 (game syllables with K)
- Activity # 12 (game syllables with W)
- Supplemental Activities

IV - 57

SCOPE FOR
READING INTERVENTION INSTRUCTION

Aprendo a leer y escribir

- **UNIT 5 (book 5)**

Week 7   **LESSON 7:** Syllables **xi, ña, ño** (10/20 minutes 4 x per week)

DAY 1
- Activity # 1
- Activity # 2 (letter formation X)
- Activity # 2 (letter formation Ñ)

DAY 2
- Activity # 5
- Activity # 6
- Activity # 7

DAY 3
- Activity # 10
- Activity # 12 (game syllables with X)
- Activity # 12 (game syllables with Ñ)
- Supplemental Activities

IV - 58

SCOPE FOR GRADE LEVEL INSTRUCTION

• UNIT 1 (book 1)

Week 1   LESSON 1: Letter **Aa** 10/15 minutes 3 x per week)

DAY 1	DAY 2	DAY 3
• Activity # 1 • Activity # 2*	• Activity # 3 • Activity # 4	• Activity # 5 • Activity # 6

Week 2   LESSON 2: Letter **Ee** (10/15 minutes 4 x per week)

DAY 1	DAY 2	DAY 3
• Activity # 1 • Activity # 2*	• Activity # 3 • Activity # 4	• Activity # 5 • Activity # 6

Week 3   LESSON 3: Letter **Ii** (10/15 minutes 4 x per week)

DAY 1	DAY 2	DAY 3	DAY 4
• Activity # 1 • Activity # 2	• Activity # 3 • Activity # 4	• Activity # 5 • Activity # 6	• A-E-I Activity

Week 4   LESSON 4: Letter **Oo** (10/15 minutes 4 x per week)

DAY 1	DAY 2	DAY 3	DAY 4
• Activity # 1 • Activity # 2	• Activity # 3 • Activity # 4	• Activity # 5 • Activity # 6	• A-E-I-O Activity

SCOPE FOR
GRADE LEVEL INSTRUCTION

• UNIT 1 (book 1)

Week 5 — LESSON 5: Letter **Uu** (10/15 minutes 5 x per week)

DAY 1	DAY 2	DAY 3	DAY 4	DAY 5
• Activity # 1 • Activity # 2	• Activity # 3 • Activity # 4	• Activity # 5 • Activity # 6	• A-E-I-O-U Activity • Activity # 10 • Activity # 13	• Activity # 11 • Activity # 12

• UNIT 2 (book 2)

Week 1 — LESSON 1: Syllables **ma, me, mi, mo, mu** (10/15 minutes 5 x per week)

DAY 1	DAY 2	DAY 3	DAY 4	DAY 5
• Video Presentation • Activity # 1 • Activity # 2	• Activity # 3 • Activity # 4* • Activity # 5 • Activity # 6 • Supplemental Activities (*) opcional	• Activity # 7 • Activity # 8 • Activity # 9 • Activity # 10 • Supplemental Activities	• Activity # 11 • Activity # 12	• Supplemental Activities • Activity # 13 • Activity # 14 • Activity # 15 • Activity # 16 • Extension Activities: card game

Week 2 — LESSON 2: Syllables **pa, pe, pi, po, pu** (10/15 minutes 5 x per week)

You follow the same teaching plan as in week 1, of Unit 2.

Week 3 — LESSON 3: Syllables **sa, se, si, so, su** (10/15 minutes 5 x per week)

You follow the same teaching plan as in week 1, of Unit 2.

SCOPE FOR GRADE LEVEL INSTRUCTION

• UNIT 2 (book 2)

Week 4 — **LESSON 4:** Syllables **ta, te, ti, to, tu** (10/15 minutes 5 x per week)
You follow the same teaching plan as in week 1, of Unit 2.

Week 5 — **LESSON 5:** Syllables **la, le, li, lo, lu** (10/15 minutes 5 x per week)
You follow the same teaching plan as in week 1, of Unit 2.

Week 4 — **LESSON 4:** Syllables **za, ze, zi, zo, zu** (10/20 minutes 4 x per week)
You follow the same teaching plan as in week 1, of Unit 2.

• UNIT 3 (book 3)

Week 1 — **LESSON 1:** Syllables **ra, re, ri, ro, ru** (10/15 minutes 5 x per week)
You follow the same teaching plan as in week 1, of Unit 2.

Week 2 — **LESSON 2:** Syllables **na, ne, ni, no, nu** (10/15 minutes 5 x per week)
You follow the same teaching plan as in week 1, of Unit 2.

Week 3 — **LESSON 3:** Syllables **ba, be, bi, bo, bu** (10/15 minutes 5 x per week)
You follow the same teaching plan as in week 1, of Unit 2.

Week 4 — **LESSON 4:** Syllables **fa, fe, fi, fo, fu** (10/15 minutes 5 x per week)
You follow the same teaching plan as in week 1, of Unit 2.

Week 5 — **LESSON 5:** Syllables **da, de, di, do, du** (10/15 minutes 5 x per week)
You follow the same teaching plan as in week 1, of Unit 2.

SCOPE FOR GRADE LEVEL INSTRUCTION

• UNIT 4 (book 4)

Week 1 — **LESSON 1:** Syllables **ca, co, cu** (10/15 minutes 5 x per week)
You follow the same teaching plan as in week 1, of Unit 2.

Week 2 — **LESSON 2:** Syllables **ce, ci, que, qui** (10/15 minutes 5 x per week)

DAY 1	DAY 2	DAY 3	DAY 4
• Activity # 1 (ce, ci)	• Supplemental Activities	• Activity # 8	• Activity # 13
• Activity # 1 (que, qui)	• Activity # 4	• Activity # 9	• Activity # 14
• Activity # 2	• Activity # 5	• Activity # 10	• Activity # 15
• Activity # 3 (ce, ci)	• Activity # 6	• Activity # 11	• Activity # 16
• Activity # 3 (que, qui)	• Activity # 7	• Activity # 12	• Supplemental Activities
	• Supplemental Activities	• Supplemental Activities	
	• Game: Syllables Memory		

Week 3 — **LESSON 3:** Syllables **ja, je, ji, jo, ju** (10/15 minutes 5 x per week)
You follow the same teaching plan as in week 1, of Unit 2.

Week 4 — **LESSON 4:** Syllables **ga, go, gu** (10/15 minutes 5 x per week)
You follow the same teaching plan as in week 1, of Unit 2.

SCOPE FOR GRADE LEVEL INSTRUCTION

• UNIT 4 (book 4)

Week 5 — **LESSON 5:** Syllables **ge, gi, gue, gui** (10/15 minutes 5 x per week)

DAY 1	DAY 2	DAY 3	DAY 4
• Activity # 1 (ge, gi) • Activity # 1 (gue, gui) • Activity # 3 (ge, gi) • Activity # 3 (gue, gui) • Activity # 4 • Supplemental Activities	• Activity # 5 • Activity # 6 • Activity # 7 • Supplemental Activities • Game: Syllables Memory	• Activity # 8 • Activity # 9 • Activity # 10 • Activity # 11 • Activity # 12 • Supplemental Activities	• Activity # 13 • Activity # 14 • Activity # 15 • Activity # 16 • Supplemental Activities

Week 6 — **LESSON 6:** Syllables **cha, che, chi, cho, chu** (10/15 minutes 5 x per week)
You follow the same teaching plan as in week 1, of Unit 2.

• UNIT 5 (book 5)

Week 1 — **LESSON 1:** Syllables **va, ve, vi, vo, vu** (10/15 minutes 5 x per week)
You follow the same teaching plan as in week 1, of Unit 2.

Week 2 — **LESSON 4:** Syllables **lla, lle, lli, llo, llu** (10/15 minutes 5 x per week)
You follow the same teaching plan as in week 1, of Unit 2.

Week 3 — **LESSON 3:** Syllables **ya, ye, yi, yo, yu** (10/15 minutes 5 x per week)
You follow the same teaching plan as in week 1, of Unit 2.

IV - 63

SCOPE FOR GRADE LEVEL INSTRUCTION ✓

Aprendo a leer y escribir

• UNIT 5 (book 5)

Week 4 — **LESSON 4:** Syllables **za, ze, zi, zo, zu** (10/15 minutes 5 x per week)
You follow the same teaching plan as in week 1, of Unit 2.

Week 5 — **LESSON 5:** Syllables **ha, he, hi, ho, hu** (10/15 minutes 5 x per week)
You follow the same teaching plan as in week 1, of Unit 2.

Week 6 — **LESSON 6:** Syllables **ki, ko, wa, wi** (10/15 minutes 5 x per week)

DAY 1	DAY 2	DAY 3	DAY 4	DAY 5
• Activity # 1 • Activity # 2 (letter formation K) • Activity # 2 (letter formation W) • Activity # 3 • Activity # 4 • Supplemental Activities: Make syllables	• Activity # 5 • Activity # 6 • Activity # 7	• Activity # 8 • Activity # 9 • Activity # 10	• Activity # 11 • Activity # 12 (game syllables with K)	• Activity # 12 (game syllables with W) • Supplemental Activities

Week 7 — **LESSON 7:** Syllables **xi, ña, ño** (10/15 minutes 5 x per week)

DAY 1	DAY 2	DAY 3
• Activity # 1 • Activity # 2 (letter formation X) • Activity # 2 (letter formation Ñ)	• Activity # 5 • Activity # 6 • Activity # 7 • Activity # 10 • Activity # 12	• Activity # 12 (game syllables with X) • Activity # 12 (game syllables with Ñ) • Supplemental Activities • Game: Syllables Memory

Aprendo a leer y escribir

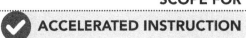

SCOPE FOR ACCELERATED INSTRUCTION

• UNIT 2 (book 2)

Week 1 — **LESSON 1:** Syllables **ma, me, mi, mo, mu** (10 minutes 4 x per week)

DAY 1	DAY 2	DAY 3	DAY 4
• Video Syllable Presentation • Activity # 1 • Activity # 2 • Activity # 3	• Activity # 5 • Activity # 8 • Activity # 9 • Activity # 10	• Activity # 11 • Activity # 12	• Activity # 13 • Activity # 14 • Activity # 15 • Activity # 16 • Supplemental Activities

Week 2 — **LESSON 2:** Syllables **pa, pe, pi, po, pu** (10 minutes 4 x per week)
You follow the same teaching plan as in week 1, of Unit 2.

Week 3 — **LESSON 3:** Syllables **sa, se, si, so, su** (10 minutes 4 x per week)
You follow the same teaching plan as in week 1, of Unit 2.

Week 4 — **LESSON 4:** Syllables **ta, te, ti, to, tu** (10 minutes 4 x per week)
You follow the same teaching plan as in week 1, of Unit 2.

Week 5 — **LESSON 5:** Syllables **la, le, li, lo, lu** (10 minutes 4 x per week)
You follow the same teaching plan as in week 1, of Unit 2.

• UNIT 3 (book 3)

Week 1 — **LESSON 1:** Syllables **ra, re, ri, ro, ru** (10 minutes 4 x per week)
You follow the same teaching plan as in week 1, of Unit 2.

SCOPE FOR ACCELERATE INSTRUCTION

Aprendo a leer y escribir

• UNIT 3 (book 3)

Week 2 — **LESSON 2:** Syllables **na, ne, ni, no, nu** (10 minutes 4 x per week)
You follow the same teaching plan as in week 1, of Unit 2.

Week 3 — **LESSON 3:** Syllables **ba, be, bi, bo, bu** (10 minutes 4 x per week)
You follow the same teaching plan as in week 1, of Unit 2.

Week 4 — **LESSON 4:** Syllables **fa, fe, fi, fo, fu** (10 minutes 4 x per week)
You follow the same teaching plan as in week 1, of Unit 2.

Week 5 — **LESSON 5:** Syllables **da, de, di, do, du** (10 minutes 4 x per week)
You follow the same teaching plan as in week 1, of Unit 2.

• UNIT 4 (book 4)

Week 1 — **LESSON 1:** Syllables **ca, co, cu** (10 minutes 4 x per week)
You follow the same teaching plan as in week 1, of Unit 2.

Week 2 — **LESSON 2:** Syllables **ce, ci, que, qui** (10/15 minutes 4 x per week)

DAY 1	DAY 2	DAY 3	DAY 4
• Activity # 1 (ce, ci)	• Activity # 5	• Activity # 11	• Activity # 13
• Activity # 1 (que, qui)	• Activity # 8	• Activity # 12	• Activity # 14
• Activity # 2	• Activity # 9		• Activity # 15
• Activity # 3 (ce, ci)	• Activity # 10		• Activity # 16
• Activity # 3 (que, qui)			• Supplemental Activities

IV - 66

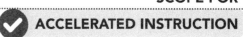

SCOPE FOR
ACCELERATED INSTRUCTION

• UNIT 4 (book 4)

Week 3 — **LESSON 3:** Syllables **ja, je, ji, jo, ju** (10 minutes 4 x per week)
You follow the same teaching plan as in week 1, of Unit 2.

Week 4 — **LESSON 4:** Syllables **ga, go, gu** (10 minutes 4 x per week)
You follow the same teaching plan as in week 1, of Unit 2.

Week 5 — **LESSON 5:** Syllables **ge, gi, gue, gui** (10 minutes 4 x per week)

DAY 1	DAY 2	DAY 3	DAY 4
• Activity # 1 (ge, gi)	• Activity # 5	• Activity # 11	• Activity # 13
• Activity # 1 (gue, gui)	• Activity # 8	• Activity # 12	• Activity # 14
• Activity # 3 (ge, gi)	• Activity # 9		• Activity # 15
• Activity # 3 (gue, gui)	• Activity # 10		• Activity # 16
			• Supplemental Activities

Week 6 — **LESSON 6:** Syllables **cha, che, chi, cho, chu** (10 minutes 4 x per week)
You follow the same teaching plan as in week 1, of Unit 2.

• UNIT 5 (book 5)

Week 1 — **LESSON 1:** Syllables **va, ve, vi, vo, vu** (10 minutes 4 x per week)
You follow the same teaching plan as in week 1, of Unit 2.

Week 2 — **LESSON 2:** Syllables **lla, lle, lli, llo, llu** (10 minutes 4 x per week)
You follow the same teaching plan as in week 1, of Unit 2.

IV - 67

SCOPE FOR ACCELERATE INSTRUCTION

• UNIT 5 (book 5)

Week 3 — **LESSON 3:** Syllables **ya, ye, yi, yo, yu** (10 minutes 4 x per week)
You follow the same teaching plan as in week 1, of Unit 2.

Week 4 — **LESSON 4:** Syllables **za, ze, zi, zo, zu** (10 minutes 4 x per week)
You follow the same teaching plan as in week 1, of Unit 2.

Week 5 — **LESSON 5:** Syllables **ha, he, hi, ho, hu** (10 minutes 4 x per week)
You follow the same teaching plan as in week 1, of Unit 2.

Week 6 — **LESSON 6:** Syllables **ki, ko, wa, wi** (10 minutes 4 x per week)

DAY 1	DAY 2	DAY 3	DAY 4
• Activity # 1 • Activity # 2 (letter formation K) • Activity # 2 (letter formation W) • Activity # 3	• Activity # 5 • Activity # 6 • Activity # 7	• Activity # 8 • Activity # 9 • Activity # 10	• Activity # 11 • Activity # 12 (game syllables with K) • Activity # 12 (game syllables with K)

Week 7 — **LESSON 7:** Syllables **xi, ña, ño** (10 minutes 3 x per week)

DAY 1	DAY 2	DAY 3
• Activity # 1 • Activity # 2 (letter formation X) • Activity # 2 (letter formation Ñ)	• Activity # 5 • Activity # 6 • Activity # 7 • Activity # 10	• Activity # 12 (game syllables with X) • Activity # 12 (game syllables with Ñ)

SECTION V

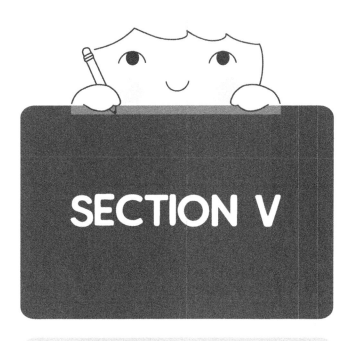

ASSESSMENT INSTRUMENT

1. Teacher's Protocol
2. Student's Protocol

Teaching Guide
Phonetic Syllabic Method

ASSESSMENT INSTRUMENT

Assessment

This is an informal, individually administered assessment instrument to help teachers diagnose their student's needs in phonics skills. This assessment tool can be used to determine where to start instruction with Aprendo a leer y escribir workbooks. It can also provide data about progress at the end of an instructional period.

This assessment presents a number of lists of syllables and words for the student to decode. Pseudowords are included since the student must use decoding skills to correctly sound out these words and cannot memorize them.

The length of time needed to administer this assessment tool will vary depending on the task at which a student begins the assessment and how many tasks the students successfully completes.

Administration

Students read from the Student Protocol on the pages that follow the Record Form. To help the student focus on the part of the test being given, it is recommended to cover the other part with a piece of paper.

The Record Form shows the same material that appears on the Student Protocol, in a reduced size, to make it easier to register the student's responses.

Stop the assessment when a student scores less than 50% on a given task.

When done with the administration, score each of the sections on the test and transfer the results to the Record Form.

Interpretation of Results

Students who score below 80% at a target syllable group will benefit from intensified instruction of that group of syllables. The use of the supplemental activities given in this guide is recommended to be used with this group of children.

Students who score between 80% and 90% at a target syllable group will also benefit from a review of those syllables/words.

Students who score above 90% at a target syllable group will be considered as that they mastered such a group of syllables.

SYLLABIC PHONICS ASSESSMENT

Syllabic Phonics Assessment
Record Sheet

• Book 1

Vowel sounds

A I O U E ☐ /5

a o u e i ☐ /5

• Book 2

Syllable decoding: m + vowel

m

me mi mo ma mu ☐ /5

Word decoding: m

mama memo mimo meme mami ☐ /5

moma mumá mamo memi mumu ☐ /5

☐ /10

SYLLABIC PHONICS ASSESSMENT

Syllable decoding: p + vowel

po pu pi pa pe   /5

p

Word decoding: m - ⓟ

papá mimo mapa mamá puma   /5

mopi pama mapo mepe pima   /5

/10

Syllable decoding: s + vowel

su so se si sa   /5

s

Word decoding: m - p - ⓢ

masa mesa suma sapo sopa   /5

supa pumo miso papo mape   /5

/10

Syllable decoding: l + vowel

lu lo li le la   /5

l

Word decoding: m - p - s - ⓛ

palo lupa lima mula sala   /5

sela limo palu sila lopa   /5

/10

SYLLABIC PHONICS ASSESSMENT

Syllable decoding: t + vowel

te to ti ta tu   /5

t

Word decoding: m - p - s - l - (t)

pato late moto toma topo   /5

poto lato tema setu topa   /5

/10

• Book 3

Syllable decoding: r + vowel

ro ru ri ra re   /5

r

Word decoding: m - p - s - l - t - (r)

ropa rama rata ruta risa   /5

rila ropo reta ruma rame   /5

/10

Syllable decoding: n + vowel

no nu ni na ne   /5

n

Word decoding: m - p - s - l - t - r - (n)

luna nota reno mano nena   /5

nula mino nato lena nona   /5

/10

V - 74

Permission granted to reproduce this page for classroom use.

SYLLABIC PHONICS ASSESSMENT

Syllable decoding: b + vowel

be ba bu bi bo   /5

Word decoding: m-p-s-l-t-r-n-ⓑ

sube bate beso nube lobo   /5

besu lobe rube taba niba   /5

/10

b

Syllable decoding: f + vowel

fo fu fa fi fe   /5

Word decoding: m-p-s-l-t-r-n-b-ⓕ

faro foto filo fila fino   /5

nofi fata fala lifa fobo   /5

/10

f

Syllable decoding: d + vowel

de di do da du   /5

Word decoding: m-p-s-l-t-r-n-b-f-ⓓ

dado dedo nudo nido duna   /5

nodo dapa lade bode duno   /5

/10

d

SYLLABIC PHONICS ASSESSMENT

Aprendo a leer y escribir

• Book 4

Syllable decoding: c + vowel   **c**

ca ce co ci cu   /5

Word decoding: m-p-s-l-t-r-n-b-f-d-c

capa cima cuna cena copa   /5

conu cina cota cafa cema   /5   /10

Syllable decoding: que - qui   **q**

qui que que qui que   /5

Word decoding: m-p-s-l-t-r-n-b-f-d-c-q

queso quise quema quena quiso   /5

peque quipo quesa tuque quino   /5   /10

Syllable decoding: j + vowel   **j**

jo ja je ji ju   /5

Word decoding: m-p-s-l-t-r-n-b-f-d-c-q-j

jefe ceja teja jota caja   /5

feje joma jata teju jifo   /5   /10

Permission granted to reproduce this page for classroom use.

Aprendo a leer y escribir

SYLLABIC PHONICS ASSESSMENT

g

Syllable decoding: g + vowel

ga ge go gu gi   /5

Word decoding: m-p-s-l-t-r-n-b-f-d-c-q-j-(g)

mago gota gema gira paga   /5
moga gepa gila mugo giru   /5   /10

Syllable decoding: gue - gui

gue gui gue gue gui   /5

Word decoding: m-p-s-l-t-r-n-b-f-d-c-q-j-(g)

Miguel guiso guisa guerra Guido   /5
guime guela mague guite pegui   /5   /10

ch

Syllable decoding: ch + vowel

chi cho cha chi chu   /5

Word decoding: m-p-s-l-t-r-n-b-f-d-c-q-j-g-(ch)

leche chile chelo coche ficha   /5
lechi chela cucha facha cholo   /5   /10

Permission granted to reproduce this page for classroom use.

V - 77

SYLLABIC PHONICS ASSESSMENT

• Book 5

Syllable decoding: v + vowel   `v`

va vi vo ve vu   /5

Word decoding: m-p-s-l-t-r-n-b-f-d-c-q-j-g-ch-v

vaca lava vino vaso pavo   /5

pave lavi vano vasa vaco   /5

/10

Syllable decoding: ll + vowel   `ll`

lle llu lla llo lle   /5

Word decoding: m-p-s-l-t-r-n-b-f-d-c-q-j-g-ch-v-ll

llave llora silla llama gallo   /5

callo llane llava galla llevu   /5

/10

Syllable decoding: y + vowel   `y`

ye ya yo yu yo   /5

Word decoding: m-p-s-l-t-r-n-b-f-d-c-q-j-g-ch-v-ll-y

yoga yate rayo soya yema   /5

yesa yogu yuco seyo maye   /5

/10

Permission granted to reproduce this page for classroom use.

SYLLABIC PHONICS ASSESSMENT

Syllable decoding: z + vowel

ze zo zu zi za   /5

z

Word decoding: m-p-s-l-t-r-n-b-f-d-c-q-j-g-ch-v-ll-y-(z)

tiza zeta zumo caza taza   /5

tozu zata teza zomo toza   /5

/10

Syllable decoding: h + vowel

ho hu hi he ha   /5

h

Word decoding: m-p-s-l-t-r-n-b-f-d-c-q-j-g-ch-v-ll-y-z-(h)

Hache hoja hada humo hilo   /5

Hama hota himo hesa huco   /5

/10

Syllable decoding: k + vowel, w + vowel

ka ki wa wi ka   /5

k-w

Word decoding: m-p-s-l-t-r-n-b-f-d-c-q-j-g-ch-v-ll-y-z-h-(k)-(w)

kiwi wifi kilo kepis kilo   /5

wifa kila pike kawa kali   /5

/10

Permission granted to reproduce this page for classroom use.

SYLLABIC PHONICS ASSESSMENT

Syllable decoding: x + vowel, ñ + vowel

xi xo ño ña ñu   /5

Word decoding: m-p-s-l-t-r-n-b-f-d-c-q-j-g-ch-v-ll-y-z-h-k-w-x-ñ

niño niña ñoqui baño caña   /5

noñi coña niñu ñani sañe   /5

/10

Aprendo a leer y escribir

Name _____ Grade _____ Date _____

Phonics Assessment Skills Summary

Book 1: a-e-i-o-u

Vowels ____ /5 ____ % uppercase
       ____ /5 ____ % lowercase

Book 2: m-p-s-l-t

Syllables ____ /25 ____ %
Words   ____ /50 ____ %

Book 3: m-p-s-l-t-r-n-b-f-d

Syllables ____ /25 ____ %
Words   ____ /50 ____ %

Book 4: m-p-s-l-t-r-n-b-f-d-c-q-j-g-ch

Syllables ____ /30 ____ %
Words   ____ /60 ____ %

Book 5: m-p-s-l-t-r-n-b-f-d-c-q-j-g-ch-v-ll-y-z-h-k-w-ñ

Syllables ____ /35 ____ %
Words   ____ /70 ____ %

Permission granted to reproduce this page for classroom use.

a   o   u   e   i

A   I   O   U   E

---

me   mi   mo   ma   mu

mamá   Memo   mimo   meme   mami

moma   muma   Memo   memi   mumu

po   pu   pi   pa   pe

papá   mimo   mapa   mamá   puma

mopi   pama   mapo   mepe   pima

su   so   se   si   sa

masa   mesa   suma   sapo   sopa

supa   pumo   miso   papo   mape

Permission granted to reproduce this page for classroom use.

lu   lo   li   le   la

palo   lupa   lima   mula   sala

sela   limo   palu   sila   lopa

✂ -

te   to   ti   ta   tu

pato   late   moto   toma   topo

poto   lato   tema   setu   topa

ro   ru   ri   ra   re

ropa   rama   rata   ruta   risa

rila   ropo   reta   ruma   rame

- ✄

no   nu   ni   na   ne

luna   nota   reno   mano   nena

nula   mino   nato   lena   nona

Permission granted to reproduce this page for classroom use.

be   ba   bu   bi   bo

sube   bate   beso   nube   lobo

besu   lobe   rube   taba   niba

fo   fu   fa   fi   fe

faro   foto   filo   fila   fino

nofi   fata   fala   lifa   fobo

de   di   do   da   du

dado   dedo   nudo   nido   duna

nodo   dapa   lade   bode   duno

--- ✂ ---

ca   ce   co   ci   cu

capa   cima   cuna   cena   copa

conu   cina   cota   cafa   cema

qui   que   que   qui   que

queso   quise   quema   quena   quiso

peque   quipo   quesa   tuque   quino

------

jo   ja   je   ji   ju

jefe   ceja   teja   jota   caja

feje   joma   jata   teju   jifo

ga　ge　go　gu　gi

mago　gota　gema　gira　paga

moga　gepa　gila　mugo　giru

- ✂

gue　gui　gue　gue　gui

Miguel　guiso　guisa　guerra　Guido

guime　guela　mague　guite　pegui

chi   cho   cha   chi   chu

leche   chile   chelo   coche   ficha

lechi   chela   cucha   facha   cholo

---

va   vi   vo   ve   vu

vaca   lava   vino   vaso   pavo

pave   lavi   vano   vasa   vaco

lle   lli   llu   lla   llo

llave   llora   silla   llama   gallo

callo   llane   llava   galla   llevu

--- ✂

ye   ya   yo   yu   yo

yoga   yate   rayo   soya   yema

yesa   yogu   yuco   seyo   maye

ze   zo   zu   zi   za

tiza   zeta   zumo   caza   taza

tozu   zata   teza   zomo   toza

---

ho   hu   hi   he   ha

hache   hoja   hada   humo   hilo

hama   hota   himo   hesa   huco

ka   ki   wa   wi   ka

kiwi   wifi   kilo   kepis   kilo

wifa   kila   pike   kawa   kali

xi   xo   ño   ña   ñu

niño   niña   ñoqui   baño   caña

noñi   coña   niñu   ñani   sañe

Student's Progress Record

STUDENT'S NAME	Book 1: A E I O U	Book 2: M P S T L	Book 3: R N B F D	Book 4: C (ca,co,cu) C (ce,ci) QUE QUI J G (ga,go,gu) G (ge,gi) GUE GUI CH	Book 5: V LL Y Z H K W X Ñ

Permission granted to reproduce this page for classroom use.

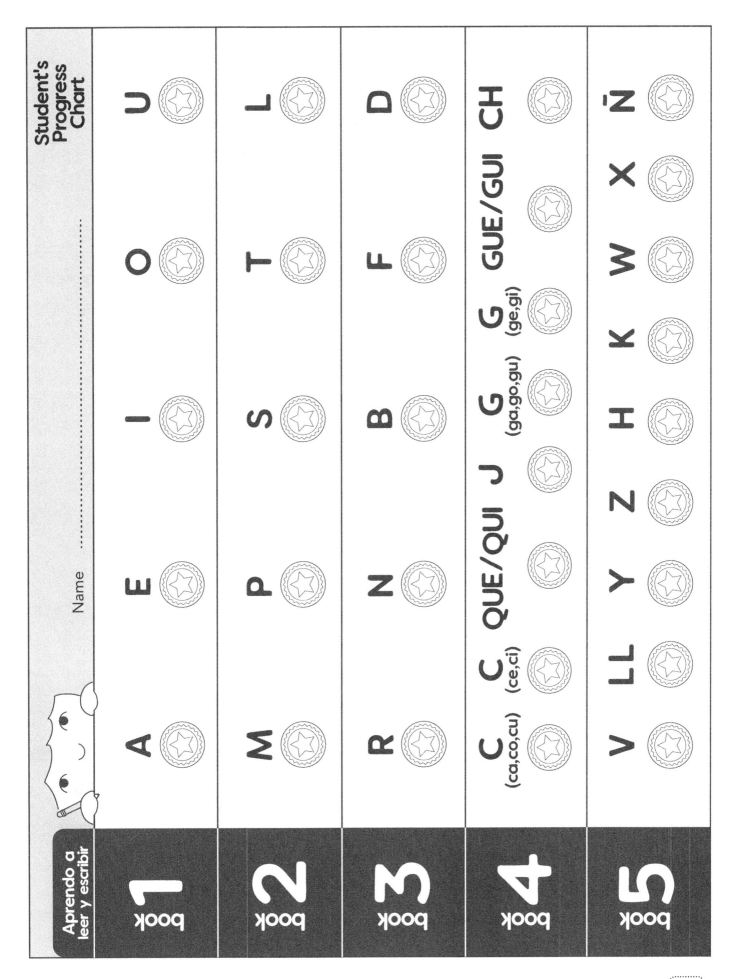

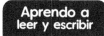

SCREENER: BOOKS 1 - 5

Name _____ Grade _____ Date _____

Screener: Syllabic phonics Assessment • Books 1 - 5
Record Sheet

- **Book 1:**

Vowels

a   e   i   o   u   ___/5   ___%

- **Book 2:**

Syllable / word decoding: m-p-s-l-t

me   pa   so   lu   ti   ___/5

mimo   puma   sapo   lima   pato   ___/5   ___/10   ___%

- **Book 3:**

Syllable / word decoding: r-n-b-f-d

ra   ne   bo   fi   du   ___/5

rata   reno   nube   foto   nido   ___/5   ___/10   ___%

- **Book 4:**

Syllable / word decoding: qu-j-g-ch

ca   ce   qui   go   ju   ___/5

coche   ceja   queso   gato   gema   ___/5   ___/10   ___%

- **Book 5:**

Syllable / word decoding: v-ll-y-z-h-k-w-x-ñ

va   zu   ki   wa   ño   ___/5

pavo   gallo   yema   tiza   hoja   ___/5   ___/10   ___%

Permission granted to reproduce this page for classroom use.

me	pa	so	lu	ti
mimo	puma	sapo	lima	pato

ra	ne	bo	fi	du
rata	reno	nube	foto	nido

ca	ce	qui	go	ju
coche	ceja	queso	gato	gema

va	zu	ki	wa	ño
pavo	gallo	yema	tiza	hoja

Permission granted to reproduce this page for classroom use.

APPENDIX BOOK 6 AND BOOK 7

APPENDIX BOOK 6 AND BOOK 7

Book 6

In **Aprendo a leer y escribir** books 1 to 5, students learn to read and write two direct syllable words. In Book 6, students review words with every direct syllable (consonant + vowel) previously learned and introduces new two, three and four-syllable words. The words repeated several times throughout the different activities, which facilitates their memorization, and thus enrichment of the child's vocabulary. Also, in Book 6, every word has an illustration as visual support to facilitate the understanding of each new read word. By the end of Book 6, the child will have learned more than 200 new words.

Book 7

Aprendo a leer y escribir, Book 7 introduces Inverse Syllables (vowel + consonant)*, Syllables with blending consonants (double consonant + Vowel)**, and Syllables with Diphthongs (the combination of two vowels in a syllable)***. In Book 7, also, every word has an illustration as visual support to facilitate the understanding of each new read word. By the end of Book 7 the child would have learned 180 new words.

After completion of books 1 to 7, students would have practiced reading and spelling all the different types of syllables that can be encountered in written Spanish.

*Inverse syllables covered in book 7: vowel + s, vowel + n, vowel + r, vowel + l, vowel + m.

**Syllables with blending consonants in book 7: pl + vowel, pr + vowel, bl + vowel, br + vowel, cl + vowel, cr + vowel, fl + vowel, fr + vowel, gl + vowel, gr + vowel, dr + vowel, tr + vowel.

***Syllables with diphthongs in book 7: ai, ia, ie, ei, io, oi, au, ua, eu, ue, iu, ui.

SYLLABIC PHONICS ASSESSMENT

Syllabic Phonics Assessment
Record Sheet

• Book 6

3 Direct Syllable words

mochila   piñata   cebolla   guitarra   número   /5

4 Direct Syllable words

limonada   lavadora   chocolate   hipopótamo   telaraña   /5

• Book 7

Reverse Syllables

os   in   er   ul   am   /5

isla   pinta   circo   pulpo   campo   /5   /10

Syllable with blending consonants

pre   bri   cla   fru   gro   /5

plato   cabra   crece   flota   tigre   /5   /10

Syllable with dipthongs

pai   via   cua   hue   rui   /5

nieve   piano   jaula   cueva   reina   /5   /10

Permission granted to reproduce this page for classroom use.

mochila   piñata   cebolla   guitarra   número

limonada   lavadora   chocolate   hipopótamo   telaraña

✂

os   in   er   ul   am

isla   pinta   circo   pulpo   campo

ple   bri   cla   fru   gro

plato   cabra   crece   flota   tigre

pai   via   cua   hue   rui

nieve   piano   jaula   cueva   reina

Made in the USA
Coppell, TX
24 June 2023

18483045R00070